PALE BLUE HOPE

PALE BLUE HOPE

Death and Life in Asian Peacekeeping

RONALD POULTON

TURNSTONE PRESS

Turnstone Press
Artspace Building
018-100 Arthur Street
Winnipeg, MB
R3B 1H3 Canada
www.TurnstonePress.com

Turnstone Press gratefully acknowledges the assistance of the Canada Council for the Arts, the Manitoba Arts Council, the Government of Canada through the Book Publishing Industry Development Program, and the Government of Manitoba through the Department of Culture, Heritage, Tourism and Sport, Arts Branch, for our publishing activities.

Excerpt on page 26 from *Central Asia, a Lonely Planet Travel Survival Kit*. Reproduced with permission from *Central Asia* 1st Edition c 1996 Lonely Planet Publications Pty Ltd.

Cover design: Jamis Paulson
Interior design: Sharon Caseburg
Printed and bound in Canada by Friesens for Turnstone Press.

Library and Archives Canada Cataloguing in Publication

Poulton, Ron, 1959-

    Pale blue hope : death and life in Asian peacekeeping / Ronald Poulton.

ISBN 978-0-88801-330-9

    1. Poulton, Ron, 1959-. 2. United Nations Mission of Observers in Tajikistan. 3. Tajikistan--Politics and government--1991-. 4. Dushanbe (Tajikistan). 5. Trials (Murder)--Tajikistan--Dushanbe. 6. Humanitarian intervention--Cambodia--Psychological aspects. 7. Lawyers--Canada--Biography.

I. Title.

DK928.867.P69A3 2009   958.608'6   C2009-900714-2

To Toni, Jack and Matthew

AUTHOR'S NOTE

The persons depicted in this book are all real people. I have changed some of their names and/or nationalities for issues of protection, or simple privacy. In addition, I have attempted to depict events as accurately as my memory would allow. I tried to get it right, but apologize for any errors made.

PALE BLUE HOPE

I.
ARRIVAL
TAJIKISTAN, 1998

A PROSTITUTE WITH HER LEGS SPREAD WIDE
(Tashkent, Uzbekistan—September 1998)

The only commercial air carrier into Tajikistan in 1998 is Tajikistan Airlines with planes that skip like stones over flat ponds of landing fields and sometimes come to rest upside down. United Nations personnel are prohibited from hanging upside down in Tajikistan Airlines airplanes, so I fly into the region on Lufthansa.

"Welcome to Uzbekistan," says the German pilot to us over the plane's loudspeaker. "Please wait until the plane comes to a stop before...." Everyone is already standing, reaching for overhead baggage, jostling for a place in line—everyone except me. Enjoying the comfort of my seat, I cling to the last moments of a familiar landscape. Waiting for me down the ramp and beyond the plane is all new ground. Once more I am about to become a stranger in a country, and I hesitate before stepping into that role again.

Tashkent, Uzbekistan is my landing pad into Central Asia and the staging area for UN operations in the region. I am to be met by our military here and then flown to Almati, Kazakhstan aboard UN aircraft and then on to my final destination of Dushanbe, Tajikistan, where my new job and my next new life awaits.

I finally leave my Lufthansa seat to join the line of men with *tupi*—the harlequin-coloured Muslim head coverings that fit snugly over the crown of their heads—and women in *rumoli* headscarves and women without either that crowd the aisle. Some of the men are in military uniform. The man nearest me, in a business suit with a cardigan underneath his jacket despite the stifling heat, already has a cigarette pulled out. He holds it between yellowed fingers and begins tapping the filtered end against the top of the seat next to where he stands. Most of the men have cigarettes in hand. One is already lighting up.

"There is a delay," the stewardess announces in English, waving her finger at the lit cigarette until the man squeezes it out between thick, stained fingers. "Please sit down." No one moves to their seats. The announcement sounds more like a plea and is repeated in Russian, then in a language I guess is Uzbek, but everyone remains standing, afraid to lose their place in line. The German stewardesses are agitated by this lack of obedience. I help them out by sitting down.

I had received cables from UN Movement Control (MOVCON) while I was still in Canada telling me that I would be met in Tashkent and taken to a hotel for the night and then into Kazakhstan and finally Tajikistan on a UN flight the next morning. I have my doubts that anyone will actually be at the airport to receive me. In preparation for being on my own in Tashkent I have brought with me enough American dollars to find a taxi and hotel. I am worried about how to locate the United Nations offices, however, with no capacity in the local languages. Finding a place to stay is merely a matter of finding a taxi, paying whatever is asked and being taken to a hotel. But, no one will know where the UN offices are, I feel sure. The operation in Uzbekistan is too small.

Once out of the plane and waiting in line for customs control, I watch as a group of Americans, on the other side of the rope in a line that leads out of the country, frenetically drag overweight baggage along the floor. Men and women with children in tow. I can see the embossed eagle on their passports—always in hand.

"Where you headed?" I call out across the rope to my fellow North Americans. One of the men stops wrestling with a large and bulging striped bag and looks up at me.

After too long a pause he says, "Back home. Stateside." His face is red and he is perspiring. The airport lounge is hot, the smell of cigarette smoke strong.

He seems guarded so I say, "I'm heading into Tajikistan. UN."

He smiles and stares at me. "We just left. We closed the embassy." He speaks quickly but openly, apparently not caring who may overhear.

"Why?" I ask.

He shrugs. "They never tell us anything. Good luck," he says over his shoulder as he pulls at his baggage. Two children run after him, gripping dolls in headlocks under their arms.

I'm not concerned by what he has told me. The US could have any number of diplomatic rationales for removing itself from Tajikistan. For one, it may have been a protest over issues of access to weapons sites of its choosing. It was believed that during the Cold War the Soviets had hidden intercontinental ballistic missiles in the mountain ranges of Central Asia, possibly Tajikistan. The US and its allies were now concerned that a warlord or *mujahed* would find a way to pack a nuclear bomb into a suitcase and board a ship. Such was the fear and the dread of the post-Soviet Union turbulence.

But that's not why the Americans are leaving.

"Their embassy is in a hotel," Asim, the Jordanian captain, tells me when I enter his car. I have actually been met at the airport. I am mildly surprised. "It is too vulnerable. Cannot be defended." He steers his way around the line of taxis at the airport.

One month earlier, in August 1998, the US military launched cruise missile attacks against al-Qaeda bases in Afghanistan and reprisals are anticipated.

Asim flicks the ashes of his cigarette out the window, then grips the cigarette between his front teeth to allow both his hands to be on the steering wheel. He is driving fast, the road dark and the curve he is on sharp. I hold on to the dashboard of the pickup. He looks at me and smiles through the grip on his cigarette. "I am a very good driver," he says to me. I am conscious of the fact that the number one cause of fatalities in United Nations missions is traffic accidents. United Nations staff, particularly military, especially Third World military, are very bad drivers. Dozens of United Nations personnel and locals have been killed in car crashes in Cambodia. In one instance, on a road frequented by our staff, peasants of a village became enraged one afternoon when a child was killed. They set upon the driver and hacked him to death with machetes. Rough and present justice.

"Tajikistan is too dangerous now," Asim says to me after taking the cigarette from his mouth to hold it out the open window. With one hand on the top of the wheel, cigarette in his other hand, he suddenly reminds me of my father driving me home in his blood-red Skylark at night after a baseball game when I was twelve. Throughout my life, sitting in a car at night inhaling the remnants of cigarette smoke being blown out a window has always triggered feelings of great comfort in me. The security and protectiveness of my father's presence. Now, despite Asim's words about fear and vulnerability, I feel oddly safe when he strikes such a familiar pose.

Asim is in Uzbekistan with a contingent of the United Nations military coordinating supplies and people entering and leaving the mission in Tajikistan. The military rotate into Uzbekistan every few months. It is considered rest and relaxation. The restaurants are safe at night, there is shopping and, most importantly, dance clubs and prostitutes abound. Tashkent has been described to me by one military observer as, for him, a prostitute with her legs spread wide.

"You are the lawyer," Asim suddenly says to me.

Unsure if he means it as an insult, I answer him briskly: "Yes, a lawyer."

"There has been much talk about your arrival. You are to solve the Garm business and De Marco too. That is what I believe." Without waiting for me to confirm what he said, Asim continues, "Once these killings are resolved we can return to our business. If not, we can go home." I feel suddenly important to the mission, though nothing of what Asim said about my job here means anything to me.

"De Marco I haven't heard of," I say. "Who is he?"

Asim flicks the cigarette out his window and pulls a new one out of his pack with his teeth.

"Well," he begins, cigarette dangling from his lips as he fumbles for his lighter, "his murder is worse, in my opinion." Lighting his cigarette, Asim takes a puff and then resumes the pose of one hand on wheel, one hand outside. "They sent the FBI even to sniff around. Too suspicious," he says. "The Tajiks ..." he shakes his head, side to side. "They are crazy...."

We then drive in silence for some minutes up Pushkin Avenue before he says, "The Uzbeks have a subway. Quite good."

"De Marco?" I remind him.

"Yes, sorry. De Marco was the head of security in Dushanbe for the UN.

He was killed last week. Shot in the head. The Tajiks say he was playing Russian roulette with his girlfriend and was unlucky." Asim laughs.

"What do we say?" I ask him.

"De Marco was foolish. He had a Tajik girlfriend who was in a crime family. Close to very bad people. *Mujahed* also inside. De Marco was killed by a jealous relation, maybe ex-boyfriend, or present boyfriend." He laughs again. "Or he was killed to send us a message that we are not wanted. Either way, murder, not roulette."

"Head of security?" I ask, incredulous. "UN security?" This I had not heard of prior to coming. Asim nods as he takes a puff.

"Why did we ask the FBI to come?"

"He was American citizen. One of their own. Four men in Garm are killed, Polish, Uruguay, Tajik, Japanese, and nothing. Dumb old De Marco dies and the FBI come."

I later learn that De Marco was found naked on his bed, a hole the size of a shot glass in his temple, his gun nearby. He was known to play games of spin-the-chamber with his life, so the fact that he may have been unlucky in a game is not too far-fetched.

"I was in Dushanbe at the time," Asim says. "At night. We all keep radios on. So you too. She comes on the radio, calling for help. Screaming. Crying. Good performance. Our men arrive at his house, other military, Civpol. They found his body. She says she was not in the room. But, cannot be...."

"Why not?"

"Blood, on her ear, they saw it and on her dress. Splatters of blood. She had to have been sprayed with blood. "

"Then she had to be with him when he was shot."

"Of course! She killed him, or someone killed him. She is gone, I am told. Disappeared. What can you do? The question really is why. If the *mujaheds* do not like you then this blue flag"—he gestures to his United Nations arm patch sewn into his lime-green Jordanian uniform—"is nothing. So we must solve this."

"Well, no one has told me anything about it," I say, risking his disappointment.

Without looking at me he says, "Really, sir? That is too strange."

I am not sure if he believes me. Military men are used to secrets and

9

expect that everyone has them. *Need to know* is not an insult, but a precondition to them taking you seriously.

"Well, I am sure someone will brief you." He turns his head to smile at me. "I think that is your job. To solve these crimes. Why else do you go into Tajikistan when no one can and others are leaving?"

In truth, I had not been briefed on either of the killings, neither those in Garm, which at least I had heard of, nor that of De Marco. I begin to think, however, that the reason I was needed in the country so quickly was to work on these cases. That was my history with the organization—investigating human rights violations, largely murder inquiries, in Cambodia. So it seems consistent with the expertise I acquired and with the UN Tajik desk officer's knowledge of my work; he and I had worked in Cambodia together. But why not tell me sooner, at least to prepare me for what was to come? Sitting back, listening to Asim as we follow Pushkin Avenue up to our hotel, the Hotel Uzbekistan, with memories of countless acts of UN ineptitude dancing in my head, I relegate this latest failure to fully inform me of my job as a simple act of forgetfulness by a bureaucracy that is overburdened and overloaded and overdone. But despite this, I begin to relish the challenge of what lies ahead.

DO SOME GOOD WORKS
(Montreal, Canada—1975, 1976)

I am the unlikeliest participant in international politics and peacekeeping. I was born in Montreal in 1959 and grew up an Anglo during a time of revolution in Quebec, a revolution that only touched me when the army pressed into the streets in October 1970 and the Anglo kids were told not to go out on Halloween if we didn't want to be kidnapped or murdered by the FLQ.

I did my Anglo duty and ripped and burned Parti Québécois signs in the 1976 election, but I had no real interest or engagement in political events, whether at home or abroad. Growing up in a harmonious English/French neighbourhood of Cartierville, I bused to the closest English Catholic school, St. Pius x Comprehensive High School, a gigantic English, Roman Catholic, largely Italian, fortress that sat in stacks of concrete on Papineau Avenue in the east end of Montreal. In 1975 as a senior I was six foot two and 140 pounds and floated like a feather above the heavy smells of salami wafting from the lunchroom. I was too skinny to be taken seriously, was a clear *mange* cake in a dark and heavy land, and crept like a frightened antelope amidst the Italian pride, clutching at my peanut butter sandwiches on

11

white bread. My delicate condition had to change; I knew it had to change. So, I took a deep breath and tried out for the football team, a team made up of boy-men who had already begun to shave and looked just like men in TV advertisements for beer or hairspray. They were giants, monkey giants, who spent hours in the locker room after showers preening hair that curled and rose from their heads like gladiators' helmets, then grew like capes down their backs.

The Falcons: a football tradition in the school of 2500 and a team I decided to be on. So I walked through the door of that gymnasium and into a world of rebuke and ridicule and pain, lots and lots of physical pain.

I ended up making the team, played flanker and defensive back, and went on in college, university—where I made a few interceptions because I was the only defensive player in the league who could catch and so was named to the 1981-82 All-Canadian team, and later to an unsuccessful tryout with the now-defunct Ottawa Rough Riders, where I played poorly, was permanently injured and then released from the team. I then became an unlikely lawyer.

That step through the gymnasium door and onto the St Pius X football team stayed with me. It was big and filled with doubt, but defining. To overcome my constant fears I had to take risks, big ones. At that moment and through a boy's lens, football seemed to be such a risk. Joining the United Nations some thirteen years later was just another risk to take, another door to walk through.

And then I became hooked on the thrills.

I have felt the adrenalin rush that comes from the sheer vertical climb of a Hercules military cargo plane and the suffocating heat inside those planes. I can find taxis that won't rip you off at Don Muang airport in Bangkok and will take you into the city through thick, black clouds of pollution and congealed traffic. I know that Mekong Thai whisky will blow your head open with a hangover the next day and that a gunshot wound from an AK-47 appears smaller than that from an M16. I understand that when you put people behind razor wire for years and feed them garbage cans loaded with undercooked chicken wings and take their hope away, they lose their humanity and start to kill each other. This I learned in Hong Kong, in Vietnamese refugee camps away from the camera shops and jade night market of the greatest shopping mall in the world.

At first the morality of the work is also compelling. The best impulses of humanity are reflected in the United Nations' missions. Negotiate peace. Bring aid. Rebuild destroyed infrastructures. It is hard, painful work, often lonely and alienating, as it is far from the familiar, always against the odds, and rarely well defined. When faced with child armies clutching double magazine AK-47s, child soldiers who do not have enough to eat and generals who have no power but for the hunger of these boys, and intransigence and stalemate and fear, working out the details of peace is more often a tedious and feckless exercise. The factions in a civil war will not easily give up their arms, disband armies, move soldiers into cantonment areas where they are vulnerable and easy targets for the other side, regardless of what treaties have been signed. On the other hand, the international community will not easily hand over millions in aid, despite what promises it made. The United Nations will rarely act outside its mandate for a country, despite the horrors that are confronted. And so the curtain of grey descends and every decision becomes the wrong decision very quickly and you find yourself often searching for some moral standard by which to judge something awful, something you have never seen before.

My ethical standards emanate largely from my Irish Catholic mother, who grew up on St. Urbain Street in Montreal in the 1920s, making Catholicism dominant in our house. We went to church and prayed to God and went to confessional and tried to think up impressive sins to shock the priests.

I served as an altar boy until the day poor old Father Penny, whose flatulence on the altar could put a tear in your eye, separated Sean Fitzgerald and me during one Sunday morning service for laughing our heads off. It started when Sean leaned over to me during the most delicate part of the mass, when wine and wafer are converted to blood and body and everyone waits dry-mouthed for a chance to crunch down on Christ's arms or legs or breast and whispered words I will never forget. "Hey," he said his eyes twinkling, "that guy in the third row." He even pointed for effect. "He looks just like Henri Richard." Number sixteen for the Montreal Canadians. The Habs. *Les Glorieux!* I chuckled once, as I recall, because the guy looked just like Richard, and then an emotional gate opened in Sean and he began to laugh, turn red, cough, and choke. All this made us laugh until we couldn't stop and Father Penny came farting over to us after carefully putting down Christ, and took Sean by the arm across the altar to a different bench. My career in God on the altar and in the cool white robes was over. So it is with God.

Somehow, the threads of Catholic moral teaching stayed with me and I saw the practice of law as a means to virtuous service in the secular domain. Needless to say, I watched a lot of *Perry Mason* and then *L.A. Law* and cried when juries came back with righteous awards against offending insurance companies. With little more thought than that, I studied law and became engaged with the immediate empowerment, answers, and reflections on morality. I then practised law and became quickly disenchanted with the greed and the lechery and the lies. Criminal clients were usually guilty and civil clients largely greedy. Everyone lied about everything. I looked for something better.

In 1988 Vietnamese refugees began pouring into Hong Kong. Camps were overcrowded, the United Nations in crisis mode. I watched this unfold from my wood-panelled office in Ottawa where I practised civil and criminal law and I knew I had to get out of Ottawa and do more than bring motions for more money for estranged spouses or negotiate plea bargains for my criminal clients.

I had followed some of the United Nations operations throughout the late 1970s and into the 1980s and had aspired to play some part in one. The ideology appeared pure: a global co-operative effort to end war and bring food and medical aid. I may have been naive to imagine it working effectively, but it was well worth the effort. I had watched TV images of crooked lines of trucks with blue flags carrying food into Ethiopia in the early 1980s and I had read accounts of the desperate operations of the UN in Southeast Asia. The Nobel Prize for Peace had been awarded to the United Nations High Commissioner for Refugees (UNHCR) in 1981 for the intellectual and physical courage of its staff. Faced with a humanitarian crisis posed by tens of thousands of boat people fleeing Vietnam, crammed into boats, mercilessly plundered by pirates, UNHCR had devised and implemented operations which saw the rescue, safe passage, and asylum for many of these people.

In his book *Quality of Mercy*, William Shawcross depicted the international response to the Cambodian refugee crisis in 1979 and how UNHCR Protection Officers risked life and limb to impede Thai military vehicles attempting to send back refugees into the land mines and the Khmer Rouge on the Cambodian side of the border. Their actions were insane and reckless and I was deeply envious. I was inspired by this bravery, compelled by the concept of international justice, and hungry for adventure. I initially joined the United Nations to be a part of this global effort. As I saw the world in 1989, the United Nations was an organization to be reckoned with and respected, for reckless heroism if nothing else.

STAY INSIDE YOUR HOTEL
(Dushanbe, Tajikistan—September, 1998)

"You should stay inside your hotel," the Austrian lawyer, Suzanne, says to me. "It is not safe for us outside." She is at the airport to greet me upon my arrival in Dushanbe. I step off the Russian Topolev transport and into a wall of hot dry air. At that moment two Russian fighter planes, parachutes jettisoned and wagging behind them, are landing single file on an adjacent runway, wings bouncing with the weight of bombs curled like fists underneath. Surrounding our plane are the hulks of other Russian warplanes. Enormous troop carriers. Helicopter gunships. Jets. They seem rusted and old. A lone telephone booth sits in an open field between runways. I stare at it through the shimmering glare.

Beyond the airport, jagged, white-capped mountains disrupt the perfect blue sky. The great walls of the prison of Dushanbe. "You will not have a chance to go into the mountains," the Austrian is saying as we careen towards the city in a Land Cruiser driven by a Uruguayan Military Observer (MILOB). With the air conditioning blasting, it feels cold. I stare out at the scenes flashing by like flip-cards, trying to absorb a sense of the country. We are travelling so fast I can barely focus on the electric buses and Lada cars that we are flying by. The few people I see are only a blur. "It is unsafe for us," she is saying. Again the phrase, *for us*. Does she mean Austrians, I wonder?

With a white-knuckle grip on a swinging handle above my window, I strain to see my new home, partially concealed by the dust and small rocks kicked up by our racing wheels. I would have preferred a slower entry into the city of Dushanbe.

Suzanne suddenly asks me, "Do you speak Russian?"

"No," I say.

She shakes her head and looks at the driver. She seems angry.

"No Russian," she repeats to herself.

"Don't we have interpreters?" I ask.

"Yes," she says, "but they are poor. It will be difficult."

Ten minutes off the plane and already I am a disappointment.

It had been five years since I last worked for the United Nations, since my entanglements in postwar Asia had kept me employed outside of Canada. In Hong Kong in 1989 for an agency paid by the United Nations High Commissioner for Refugees (UNHCR), I represented Vietnamese asylum seekers in their bid to extricate themselves from British-built razor-wire camps in the territories, and access the West, and freedom. From those camps in Hong Kong I moved to Bangkok and then into Cambodia, with one of the largest and most ambitious peacekeeping operations in history, the United Nations Transitional Authority for Cambodia (UNTAC). Here I helped establish the human rights mechanisms for investigation and corrective measures and worked as an investigator of the more serious human rights violations. Political assassination became my specialty.

In 1993 I left Cambodia and the United Nations after the first elections in Cambodia in over twenty years. I decided I had had enough of international work and I had the sense that everything that happened, everywhere, was because the United States government wanted it so. I was also homesick for Canada and tired of food poisoning and no electricity and the instability of life in the peacekeeping field. I needed to be closer to my family than a twenty-two-hour plane flight. I also needed to feel safe—which meant I was tired and ready for the first world again.

I resigned from the United Nations and made my way home.

But then some five years later, in the spring of 1998, I was working as an immigration lawyer in Toronto when a call from New York and a United Nations Desk Officer for Tajikistan yanked me up and out of my complacent life. After Cambodia it had taken me years to resettle in Canada. As so many UN personnel before me and since, I returned home and landed hard. I found myself without a job, seemingly unemployable and outside the loop of social lives that had grown since I had gone to work abroad. The practice of law is often a conservative and sterile profession, a jealous mistress that in this case didn't want to take me back.

Finally, with time, I found my way and paid my professional and social dues and remade my community. The killing fields of Cambodia were then five years behind me and I had become safely embedded in our culture. I golfed with my buddies, played hockey once a week, saw movies, went to dinner parties and discussed wines, food, local politics, sports. I didn't need to be a peacekeeper then.

I made the decision to go to Tajikistan and return to the United Nations one night, several weeks after the initial call from New York, as I sat on the rooftop of my apartment above Parliament Street in Toronto. I was watching the lights in the downtown bank towers, blinking at me. My thoughts turned to my father and his admonition never to volunteer for anything. This from a man who ate pure lard to put on enough weight to make it to the war in Europe in 1942. I never asked him why he was so against volunteering. The war turned out fine for him, a defining moment that he was proud of in his silent, humble manner. A generation of humble men, our dads were.

My dad and his friends came back from that war, one that still staggers the mind with the sheer dimensions of its horror, and then they took a couple of weeks off and went out and found jobs, put their heads down, and worked like hell for the rest of their lives until their children grew up, became teenagers and started cracking jokes about the way they drove, and then for an instant these old men were again on the beach at Juno or in a bomber at night shooting at a German night fighter. I can kill you, son, my father's eyes said to me once when I was sixteen and a constant pain in his neck. I knew at that moment that he could, and perhaps he had killed from that gunsight on the Lancaster bomber he flew into Germany during the war. It made the teen years a lot easier knowing your father could actually kill you if you pushed too hard.

"You might find it interesting," said the message on my voice mail from Adrian Verheul, the man responsible for monitoring the world's response to Tajikistan from his desk in New York. *Interesting*. The word hung in my thoughts. The work had always been interesting, but was it worth the personal cost to me, to leave again, to cut myself adrift from a place that had so reluctantly just taken me back? Was it worth the cost of again confronting the dangers, frustrations, and sorrows of peacekeeping work?

At my last posting in Cambodia in 1993, the UN had deployed some 20,000 soldiers, police, and civilians. We had control of the military, police, and government. We had tanks and helicopters and the full support of the Security Council and Member States. And yet, so many deaths occurred under our watch. A fourteen-month-old Kru Khmer baby, Lim Sou, was one, shot by the boys of the Khmer Rouge and left to linger and die. He had been, for me, a turning point. Human rights work required muscle, and weapons to defend the innocent, I came to believe. It was a belief forged by the anger I felt in looking down at a baby.

Wide-eyed and panting through fear and pain, his little cherub face looked up at me as I approached his hospital bed, lying in a row of other rusting beds, in a ward of crumbling walls, a thick congregation of flies and the putrid smell of rotting flesh and rancid ointments in the air. Lim's aunt sat beside him, fanning away the flies and trying to keep him cool. She was crying, her head bent away from me and her face buried in her red peasant's scarf, the *krama*, to conceal her tears.

In a heat that was thick and pungent, I stood at the end of Lim's bed with sweat dripping down my face and back. My mouth went dry and I couldn't breathe. *Help me*, Lim's eyes said to me. *I can't*, I blinked back through the sweat.

And so I sat on my roof that night in 1998, contemplating downtown Toronto, the constant struggle to make ends meet, my mounting debts, the offer to return to peacekeeping work, the sorrows of that work but also its exhilarations.

Then another night came to mind. A black, moonless night, years earlier. I had been riding in a United Nations French military Puma helicopter over Khmer Rouge territory in northern Cambodia. The running lights on the helicopter were off and the crew wore night-vision goggles to see and employed a device to mask the sound of the engine and the blades. If detected, we would be shot at. The helicopter had been sent from Phnom Penh to retrieve me and a team of investigators from a remote outpost where a murder had occurred. As the Puma swooped low so the pilots could find the Tonle Sap River leading into Phnom Penh, dogs barked at something in the sky they couldn't see but thought they sensed.

The thrill of that night and the importance of the work finally combined with my own innate restlessness and punctured the inertia that had taken over my life in Toronto. There were bigger problems in the world than the defect in my golf swing.

The Austrian lawyer is telling me that days before my arrival in the city an opposition political leader, Otakhon Latifi, was assassinated in broad daylight. He was a moderate in the United Tajik Opposition and in this war of extremes he was a peacemaker. Approached outside his home one morning, he was embraced by his assassin, kissed on the cheek, and then shot. His support for secularism makes his killing a major blow to the Peace Accord, Suzanne says. She is visibly shaken by this event, and her lip trembles when she tells me.

We arrive at the hotel. Suzanne turns in her seat and says, "I did not expect you. When I was told yesterday to prepare a briefing note and to pick you up, frankly, I was surprised. UN personnel are not permitted into the region now because of the insecurity, so I am a little shocked you are here. In fact, we may be evacuating. Don't unpack."

Welcome to Tajikistan.

I am handed a briefing note and told that an armoured personnel carrier will pick me up the next morning to take me to the UN offices. Suzanne surveys me head to toe and says, "You look Russian. That also puts you at risk. Please, don't leave the hotel. They have CNN. Watch TV. Enjoy your day." Then she is gone. I watch the Land Cruiser disappear into the city, a city with scatterings of people walking the streets, few cars, and a haunting presence of danger rising with the heat. Russian warplanes, assassinations, fear. I am at that moment as far as I can possibly be from my bourgeois life in Canada.

Inside the Hotel Tajikistan I find a clerk who speaks English and he arranges my room, exchanges my dollars to rubles, and explains the workings of the hotel. The women sitting on chairs by the elevator at each floor clean the rooms and sell drinks, he tells me. The hotel is very safe, he adds, but stay inside the fence.

He is a small, slight man with wild black eyebrows that sprout vigorously from his brow. He has curly black hair, cut short, and a large, slightly bent nose that angles out over a thick black moustache. The Persian ancestry of the Tajik people is clear in each of his features but one. His eyes are a piercing deep blue. The contrast is remarkable and unexpected. I cannot help but stare into his blue eyes. He is from the Pamir mountains, I later learn, in central Tajikistan, called Bam-I-Dunya, roof of the world. Some Pamiris have blue eyes because they live next to the sky, I am told by a city dweller.

This mountain man is excessively polite to me and helpful. I will spend three weeks in his hotel and each time he sees me after our first encounter he rushes to shake my hand in the double-clasp grip used by Tajiks and their Muslim cousins, and asks if everything is fine. He is never interested in why I am in Tajikistan or in anything about my home. He is content that I have chosen to be in his country now and needs no further information about me.

It is a refreshing attitude of the Tajik people that I will encounter repeatedly in my stay—their lack of fascination with the occidental tourist. In Southeast Asia I was swarmed at every turn. In a remote Cambodian village I had entered with UN police on a hunt for the murderer of a local opponent of the ruling party, a large group of women and children began forming around me. They pointed and laughed, none too discreetly, apparently at my face. Finally overcome by insecurity, I asked my interpreter, Kiempo, to wade in and inquire. He asked the crowd and was answered by a roar of more laughter. Suddenly turning red he looked at me and said, "Sorry, Ron. But it is your nose. They laugh at how long your nose is." A sea of flat button noses bobbed around me.

The Tajiks don't seem curious or hostile to outsiders, only cynical. Arab invaders arrived in the seventh century and pushed the Tajiks east from the Zeravshan valley in what is now Uzbekistan. The Turks came next in the tenth century, then the Mongols, and in the fifteenth century Tamerlane arrived. The Russians had been the most recent to come but they too were finally leaving. So the fact that I am with the United Nations or from the West is of no interest to the Tajiks. As far as they are concerned, I am just another outsider, here to take what I can and then leave.

After checking in, I enter a four-by-four-foot elevator to ride to my floor. I share the cramped space with two expensively dressed, very polite members of the Aga Khan's delegation and a Russian military officer, vodka bottle in hand. I have arrived on the weekend of the Aga Khan's visit to Tajikistan. The living god is among us in Dushanbe. His people, the Ismailis, are now nestled in this remote corner of the *former* Soviet empire, in the Pamir mountain range. The Ismailis have been on the run for centuries. They have run for their lives through the deserts of Central Asia, been pursued and hunted and persecuted as the outcasts of Islam. At first the isolation of the Pamir mountains saved them, and then with the Russians and their food supplies gone from the crumbling Soviet empire, the Pamir mountains began to kill them. Only in 1992 did the Aga Khan reconnect with this lost tribe of the Ismaili people. His emissaries came bringing food and education and his photograph. In September 1998, he left his stable of racing stallions in France and he came to Dushanbe. We arrived at the same time, he and I, into the sorrow of Tajikistan.

The war started in 1992, but had its spark from the implosion of the Russian empire in 1989 and the country's self-proclaimed independence in 1991. Remember the scenes: the Berlin Wall being hammered at; Gorbachev smiling; Reagan beaming. The Cold War was over and the US had won. The world celebrated.

Not the whole world. In Tajikistan people held their breath and wondered where their gas would come from or who would repair their generators, teach their children or set their broken bones. With the empire in disarray, many of those Russians wealthy enough to leave were returning to the motherland of Russia and taking their knowledge with them. Members of the exalted party were suddenly the former communists. The opposition in Tajikistan emerged quickly from among the liberal democrats and Muslim clerics; they united, and seized power. People stood in the streets of Dushanbe and cheered.

But the former rulers were not finished. Tajikistan is divided into regions separated by distinct geographical boundaries cutting off one area from the

23

next. Mountains, valleys, rivers. The south, the Kulyabi region, is populated by a tough agrarian population of Tajiks. They are known for their ability to fight. The central east is the Islamic heartland. The Aga Khan's people and others cling to the rock faces there. The north is Leninobod province (formerly called Leninabad), with the country's largest Uzbek population, a sector with strong ties to Uzbekistan, pro-communist sentiments and a history of opposition to those of the central and eastern zones.

In the 1930s, the Russians adopted the British tactic of "divide and conquer" and handed the reins of power to the northerners from Leninabad. In 1992, with their reign dissolving, the northern Leninobodis enlisted the southern Kulyabis for help against Islamic fundamentalism and a perceived emerging theocracy. The Uzbek and Russian military joined in against Islam.

The threat of a fundamentalist uprising was grossly exaggerated by the Russians. The coalition government of Tajik political parties in power in Tajikistan in 1992 was dominated by a secular ideology proposing democratic reforms within a secular state. Only one of the political parties in the coalition, the Islamic Renaissance Party (IRP), espoused a more fundamentalist ideology. In 1992, the IRP was a minority voice and held little sway over the direction of the coalition in power.

Rallying against this perceived fundamentalist threat and supported by Russian armour and aircraft, armies from the north and south converged on Dushanbe, the capital, and ousted the coalition government. But this was not enough. The armies then chased the opposition east and south and tried to kill every last one of them and subdue their families. In an act of inspired hatred and savagery, they released from prison a convicted mass murderer named Sangak Safarov and gave him an army. He ran amok, killed thousands, and finally frightened his own side enough for them to have him killed.

The coalition of reformers and Islamists then fled into Afghanistan, Garm (located in the central highlands of Tajikistan), and Gorno Badakhshan in the east and south.

In Garm they held the line against the onslaught while the former communists, the Leninobodis and Kulyabis took power in Dushanbe. The war festered and lingered on. Russian troops stayed and bought drugs along the Afghan border. The United Nations arrived to broker peace.

I open the standard briefing note Suzanne has given me and immediately begin reading about Team Garm. In July 1998, two months before my arrival, a United Nations observation team stationed in Garm was ambushed and all four of its members murdered. It was one of the worst murders of United Nations personnel in the organization's history. A cold-blooded killing aimed at chilling United Nations operations and disrupting the peace process, the note says. Three opposition soldiers have been arrested for the killing. My job is to follow the government's investigation and, if it happens, to observe the trial of the three accused.

The killing of peacekeepers is, tragically, not uncommon. I have been in United Nations operations before and know the hazards. While I was in Cambodia eighty-two UN personnel were killed, including the first Japanese soldiers to enter peacekeeper duties (they had been previously disentitled because of their constitution, crafted by the United States after the Second World War). Land mines, car accidents, malaria, food poisoning, assassination—these are the risks of the trade.

Given the known hazards of the work, I am mildly surprised to be told that the loss of four of our colleagues has caused such concern. The note says that all of our military personnel, distributed throughout the country to monitor the demobilization and the ceasefire, have been recalled to Dushanbe. Movement out of and throughout the city is prohibited. I will later be instructed that we must live within a six-block radius of our offices, a complex consisting of one large Sovietesque building and metal portable trailers in which most of us work. The compound is surrounded by barbed wire and guarded by two layers of security personnel. We are required to be in our apartments, steel outer door locked, by 6 p.m. each night. At 9 p.m. we are called on hand-held radios by the security chief. If there is no answer, an armed detachment of police and security is dispatched to the apartment. Under no circumstances are we to answer our front doors to anyone but other UN personnel.

Apparently this is a dangerous place. But what is the true nature of the danger? I search through the briefing note for answers, anticipating that this is futile. Sadly, but frequently in my experience, the last ones to understand what is really happening in a country are members of the United Nations. As I suspected, the note is heavily detailed with numbers and graphs and listings of factions—but explains nothing. Anticipating this problem, I have come prepared with a book that will shed more light than any report prepared by my colleagues in the United Nations.

I open my book, *Central Asia, a Lonely Planet Travel Survival Kit*, and read:

> The collapse of local economic conditions, with resulting poverty and unemployment, has created widespread desperation, and street crime is a very real problem. The police are completely ineffective and, according to what we were told, they are as likely to rob you as to help.
>
> You are safe enough during the day but do not go out after dark. Foreigners are soft, lucrative targets. Expats carry radios to call for help and even hardened New Yorkers don't venture out without Mace. If you do have to go out at night, order a taxi and arrange to be picked up at your hotel. Don't try to flag down a car on the road as it's unlikely that anyone with decent intentions will stop. (On our night of arrival, not knowing any better, we approached a battered old Lada stopped at a traffic light, only to speedily retreat when we saw that the driver was absorbed in trying to jam a cartridge into the revolver in his hands.)

I decide that for tonight I will stay in the hotel.

TEAM GARM
(Garm, Tajikistan—July 1998)

Garm was a critical area to the peace process in Tajikistan. Located in the Qarategin valley, approximately 200 kilometres northeast of Dushanbe at the edges of the Pamir mountain range, its population of some 10,000 with their distinct clan identity had supported the Islamic opposition in the civil war. When that opposition made its stand against the Russian, Uzbek, and Kulyabi onslaught in 1993, it was in Garm that they did it, fighting off the helicopters and jets and tanks with their hand-held weapons and their blood loyalties. Garm was a sacred place to the opposition. For the Russians, it was Afghanistan revisited.

The Islamic opposition fighters now roamed the mountainous terrain of this region largely unhindered by government soldiers. Their families and clans lived here. Clan loyalties were burned into their skin by the fifty-plus heat of summer and frozen into their hearts by the minus-thirty winters. Food was scarce. On the barren slopes surrounding Garm, there was no escape from the heat or cold. Trees cannot grow there. Only humans and donkeys can live, growing hard and twisted like the roots of the scraggy bushes that dot the mountains.

A strategy often used in peacekeeping is to place small teams of unarmed UN personnel into critically important areas to monitor the implementation of a peace agreement. These teams become the eyes and ears of the UN Security Council, as they are closest to the front line of the conflict and can report on ceasefire violations and the progress of troop demobilizations. They are often in remote areas, isolated, and vulnerable. They are unarmed to ensure they pose no threat.

The United Nations team in Garm comprised four men. Major Ryszard Szewczyk, a fifty-year-old military officer from Poland, was the leader of the Garm station and the most experienced international member of the team. Major Adolfo Scharpegge, a thirty-eight-year-old military officer in the Uruguayan army, had been in Tajikistan three weeks at the time of his murder. Yutako Akino, a political officer on secondment from the Japanese government, was forty-eight, a fluent Russian speaker, and a scholar specializing in Central Asia. Jourajon Mahramov, from Tajikistan, was the team's interpreter. He was forty-seven years old and from the Garm region. He had served with the UN for four years.

The interpreter's role in the UN is key. Translating the language is the lesser part of the job, translating the politics and culture the more important. Most UN officials I have known, and in fact the system as a whole, never appreciated this role and so treated interpreters as necessary baggage. Local interpreters in Tajikistan were paid approximately US $200 per month, a good salary in the country. The people they were translating for, the international staff, earned between US $4000 and $6000 per month.

Jourajon, the Garm interpreter, would have known the soldiers living in and around his area. He would have understood the dangers on the road and how best to avoid them. He would have known not to stop for armed *mujahed* fighters along an empty road, as the Garm vehicle apparently did. He would have known not to get out of a vehicle if these fighters ordered it. It appears, however, that that was exactly what Team Garm did.

The job of the UN team was to monitor the return of Tajik opposition fighters from Afghanistan to assembly areas in the Garm region where, according to the Peace Accord, they were to hand in their weapons, be counted, and then incorporated into the government structures, including the military. Most peace agreements have such conditions for demobilizing non-government soldiers. As long as soldiers continue to function under chains of command, peace remains elusive. Those chains must be broken. Trust and international presence are the ingredients for this, but these factors can only go so far in alleviating suspicions and anxieties. The armies are extremely vulnerable during this process and highly reluctant to comply. And in fact they rarely do.

In the assembly areas around Garm, everything went wrong from the start. The soldiers returning from Afghanistan to the Qarategin valley found assembly areas that lacked food, shelter, and a serious international presence. The repatriated guerrilla fighters, a battle-hardened group, grew more and more frustrated as they waited in the open, exposed. UN agencies that were supposed to bring food did not. UN agencies that were supposed to provide shelter failed to do so.

Team Garm was faced daily with appeasing the growing resentment of the opposition military leaders, who themselves had convinced soldiers under their command to return to Tajikistan and to end their fighting. They felt betrayed by the UN. They were angry.

During the spring and summer of 1998, the situation in Garm was tense. Team Garm sent regular cables to UN HQ in Dushanbe expressing concern for their safety. They had been repeatedly threatened, one such cable said. The UN had to do something about the conditions in the assembly areas.

The cables sat in a neat stack at UN HQ.

On July 20, 1998, Team Garm went missing.

On the morning of July 21, the mangled wreckage of their vehicle bearing license number UNMOT 61, was spotted at the base of a cliffside road outside of Tavildara, in the Garm area.

The bodies of all four men were strewn across the cliff face.

The Tajik government's immediate reaction was to blame the UN personnel for their bad driving habits.

Each of the men had been shot in the head and chest, execution style.

The peace process was suddenly brought to a halt.

UNENFORCEABLE PEACE

(Dushanbe, Tajikistan—September 1998)

Peace agreements are negotiated texts that set political terms to the settlement of an armed conflict. However, they are much more than just agreements to stop fighting, disband armies, exchange prisoners, and conduct elections. At their foundations lie compromises between parties who don't want to compromise but know they have no choice. If they had a choice they would wipe out their enemy and rule like kings. Instead, they bargain and seek international aid, and the United Nations responds by brokering an agreement, having it signed, and then, while the ink is still wet, the parties search for ways to wipe out the other side and rule like kings.

The United Nations can't stop wars. No amount of negotiation or outside intervention will initially resolve anything, once blood is shed. Brothers, cousins, wives, sons, and daughters have been killed. Constituencies of victims cry for more blood and drive the pace of both war and peace. Leaders know that after the first person is killed in a war it becomes a war of revenge that may continue indefinitely. Truth is not the first casualty of war, forgiveness is.

The peace agreement in Tajikistan arose because there was no decisive

31

victory and the opposition continued its fight largely from across the border in Afghanistan. So the puppet masters, Uzbekistan and Russia, grew anxious. Too much mayhem, too much Muslim brotherhood, too many Central Asian cousins to be tempted. Peace and compromise became an option only because of the fear of the war spreading throughout the region, of Islam being awakened against former communists in power in Uzbekistan, Kazakhstan, Turkmenistan, and Kyrgyzstan. Russia and Uzbekistan agreed to commit to a peaceful resolution of the conflict and so began negotiations between the government in power in Dushanbe led by Emomali Rakhmanov, a Kulyabi from the south, and an opposition now largely dominated by the Islamic Party, the lone faction to retain a military arm. Three agreements were signed between 1994 and 1997: Ceasefire, Demobilization, Election. Together they made up the General Agreement on Peace and Reconciliation, a framework for peace negotiated by the United Nations and all parties concerned. To ensure compliance and enforcement under United Nations auspices, negotiators inserted this clause: "This treaty shall be registered with the United Nations Secretariat pursuant to article 102 of the United Nations Charter and thereby enforceable under UN sanction." An appropriate insertion. How else can a peace agreement be enforced if not by the United Nations under its various mechanisms and bodies, such as the International Court of Justice and Security Council?

However, the drafters of the Peace Accords had made a fundamental mistake. The agreements signed by the Tajik combatants could not be registered with the UN and were therefore not enforceable. Only governments of recognized countries to an international agreement could compel the UN to enforce a treaty. The Tajik combatants were factions within a state, not state parties. This factor rendered the Tajik Peace Accords unenforceable by the UN.

"We will take this to the International Court," I heard opposition leaders exhort as the government continued to stall and obfuscate on the implementation of the agreement. "We will ask the UN to compel action!" It was a common cry during the tense months of attempting to put into action the terms of the documents. "Article 102!" they exclaimed in reference to the enforcement section of the UN Charter.

I remember sitting in meetings with the United Tajik Opposition (UTO) hearing this, knowing the agreements were legally meaningless, and thinking that maybe we should tell them. They had to be informed that their agreement was not a treaty and that, even if it were, the International Court of Justice could not take jurisdiction, as it hears complaints only by states; indeed, states that have agreed in advance to have disputes adjudicated by the court. I suggested this to my superior, a former military officer in the Indian army, shortly after my arrival in Tajikistan.

He cocked his head and sucked air through his teeth and then sat in a deepening silence. He began shuffling papers on his desk and said, "They probably know." He pulled at his lower lip. "It's not for us to say."

"But UN negotiators put that clause in. We told the parties it could be enforced by us without anything further. Didn't we?"

"Well, it can't," he said with a smile.

"Then what's the point? We have no power here. Legal power at least."

"This is politics," he said.

"Politics?"

"Politics," he said. "The technicalities of law have little place in politics, Ronald. At least politics at this level, on the international stage. Although I do acknowledge its relevance, of course." He nodded to me as though that concession had been made for my benefit as a lawyer.

He continued. "But listen to me. Our power comes not from the rule of law, so to speak, but from the desire for peace. The rest is just a story," he said, pointing to the peace agreement in my hand, the agreement I had begun to study in an attempt to understand the parameters of what we were supposed to be doing.

"But, the parties seem to think that these documents have some authority," I said. "Shouldn't we tell them we made a mistake?"

He paused and stared at me—a long pause. "Did we?" he finally asked, eyebrow arched, lower lip extended.

"Well, the opposition signed that thing and agreed to disband their armies and hand over weapons because they believed we would enforce the agreement." I felt I was on strong ground on this point.

"Did they? Did they really?" he asked. He waved me off as I began to answer. "They signed. That's what we needed. That's what they needed. That's what their backers needed. The fighting had to stop."

"But it hasn't," I said.

"On paper it has," he said. "And in fact it has largely abated."

"What is our role, then, if enforcement is illusory?" I asked.

"To show the flag," he said. "Maintain an international presence. Give them an avenue for peace. That kind of thing."

We are nothing here, I realized. Just warm bodies, symbolizing peace and the international community. But I didn't say this to him.

"Thank you," I said at last. " I understand."

He seemed genuinely pleased. "Yes. Good. I'm glad," he said and lowered his head to do paperwork. "Let's keep this to ourselves for now."

"Of course, sir," I said.

"Goodbye," he said.

"Goodbye."

The United Nations Mission of Observers in Tajikistan (UNMOT) was established by United Nations Security Council Resolution 968 of 16 December 1994. Its job was to monitor the implementation of the peace agreement, investigate cease-fire violations, provide *good offices* as set out in the Agreement of September 1994, and to maintain close contact with the parties to the conflict. But Resolution 968 did not provide for any enforcement by the UN. Into the field of Tajikistan went teams of United Nations peacekeepers. At first only military arrived, but as the *good offices* role grew with the continuing inability of the parties to compromise and implement terms, civilian political, electoral, and legal officers arrived—along with their entourage of support staff. As of 1998, 170 civilian staff and 33 military personnel made up UNMOT.

Dozens of white vehicles with black and blue UN markings arrived, as did helicopters and planes. The Security Council, with its powerful members, was behind it all. They had sent in the blue helmets and flags and authorized a legally *unenforceable* peace agreement.

The game of ending wars is, of course, largely politics. International muscle is subtle when NATO warplanes are out of range. Parties are cajoled, feted, bribed by the community of nations. Aid and legitimacy are often the currency. Allegiance and peace are the commodities. At first, it hardly ever works. There is too much hatred, distrust. Too many generals and warlords need the conflict to continue in order to maintain armies. Bandits flourish in post-conflict situations. There are a lot of bumps along the way to peace.

But there must be one clear imperative sustaining a UN effort. The agreement one seeks to implement must not only be legally binding but also enforceable under international law. The United Nations and community of nations are supposed to act in accordance with law. The agreement ending the war in Tajikistan was neither binding nor enforceable. It was a paper bag, bottom greasy with spilled fat, ready to split open and drop its contents.

Into the field of Tajikistan armed with this paper agreement, United Nations personnel sought to enforce the legally unenforceable.

II.
LIFE AND DEATH IN TAJIKISTAN

MY CLEANING LADY

(Dushanbe, Tajikistan—September 1998)

My hotel in Dushanbe, Tajikistan in September 1998 is ringed by a white painted metal fence and sits on a slight elevation of ground overlooking the road. Armed guards stand on the steps into the hotel. They smile at me when I walk outside. The hotel feels safe enough, but beyond the gates, in the road, I imagine that the few cars that are rolling slowly past, windows tinted and closed despite the thirty-plus heat, contain a cabal of agents eyeing me through the dark glass and deciding whether they should try for a shot now or wait until I make my way to the street. As I watch one such Lada moving slowly past my refuge and vantage point, another flies by, window open, the barrel of a gun protruding. I move back off the steps and motion to one of the hotel guards to look. I cannot speak a word of Tajik or Russian so I look at him and point to the road. Confused at first, he finally follows my outstretched arm to where I am pointing, then looks back at me, smiles and shrugs his shoulders.

I look from the slow-moving Lada to the gun-jutting speedier one now further down the road to the security guard, and decide to move back into the hotel lobby.

"Mr. Poulton," a voice calls to me from across the lobby.

I turn to see a tall, red-haired man striding purposefully towards me. I recognize him from my arrival at the airport. He is a compatriot working in the UN motor pool. He services vehicles and arranges logistics for the movement of personnel.

"Gary," he introduces himself, hand outstretched. Gary was an officer in the Canadian military before chucking it all for peacekeeping. He maintains a soldier's bearing, however, starting with the cropped hair.

"We tried calling your room, but could not get through. Telephones are useless in this country."

I notice he is carrying a hand-held radio. "I need one of those," I say to him.

"You'll get one soon enough," he says. "Not that you civilians know how to use them." His face breaks open with a wide smile. "Listen," he continues, smile intact, "I'm to tell you that we have a car, well, armoured car actually, coming for you. Be here in half an hour. You have a meeting to make, I understand, so we'll pick you up."

"Great," I say.

"Right, see you later. I have to get back to HQ." He turns to leave and I stop him.

"Wait," I say. "Why don't I just go with you? You drove, right?"

He stops and turns to me. "No," he says, smile again breaking out over his face, "I walked."

"Walked? Isn't it dangerous?"

He shrugs at me in much the same way as the hotel guard had done. "You'll find out," he says, then skips on out the door and down the steps into the street.

When my ride finally appears, it is a lumbering hulk of a vehicle with riveted steel panels and thick, bulletproof glass—an armoured car. I get in and feel the suffocating heat. The driver, a local Tajik staff member, is sweating.

"No air-con," says the driver, seeing my face and offering his answer. A small fan has been installed over the driver's side. I slide in beside my driver, my chauffeur, for the two-kilometre ride to work. The old and torn leather seats are uncomfortable in the heat. A long, knob-handled gearshift sticks up from the floor. Narrow windows, sealed shut, are pitted with bullet markings. The armoured car grinds and waddles like a tank.

"Do you get shot at? In the city?" I ask the driver, rubbing my finger along the inside of the window opposite the bullet pockmarks on the outside.

He looks at me and uses a paw of a hand to wipe a handful of sweat from his face.

"No," he says, "not in city of Dushanbe."

"Good to know," I say, trying to sound relaxed.

He eyes me and says, "Everywhere else. We are shot at. But not here, too much." There is not a trace of a smile on his face. I force a smile and a half laugh. He waggles his head at me.

Along the route to our office, I hungrily absorb as much as I can of the city. The armoured car moves so slowly that I have an opportunity to survey the life outside the compounds. I am becoming increasingly afraid I will not have a chance to see more than glimpses of a Muslim society beyond the security boundaries.

The driver takes us onto the main road. I clear away the steam that has gathered on my window and peer through at the road bustling with cars and people and animals. Horses, adorned with fine, crafted high-backed saddles and donkeys carrying loads of thatch compete with Ladas and Volgas, the proletarian cars, and micro vans, electric buses, and motorcycles. The buses lumber along the pitted roads and teeter around corners. Insect-like antennae linked to the wire cables overhead spark and sizzle as they reach their limits of contact, and then, every so often, dislodge, bringing a bus to a complete stop. I watch one such bus as passengers quickly disembark, hustle to the rear of the bus and grasp onto a rope that hangs behind. I see that the rope is attached to the electrical cables that have become dislodged. A number of these passengers, now impromptu bus workers, pull on the rope until the bus antennae are directed back onto the overhead cables that crackle and spark again. The bus moves on, leaving behind those too slow to rush back on.

Some of the people on the broken sidewalks, in the road, on the buses, re-mind me of the cartoon images of Sinbad the sailor and the Arabian nights, which, until now, have been my only reference points for historical Islam. Old men with long, grey crinkly beards bristling from their chins stroll in knee-length boots, wearing purple or black long quilted *chapan* coats and

41

square black and white *tupi* hats. These, I will come to learn, are the Tajik elders. Muslim prayer beads in hand, they are old men, looking over their shoulders to the past, still whispering the names of their great Basmatchi heroes of the 1920s, who flowed down from the mountains like the torrents of the rivers and fought the Bolsheviks for supremacy of their land and, for a while, won.

The Tajik women are adorned in long gold-threaded dresses and head-scarves, Day-Glo slippers on their feet. These women are sprinkled through-out the city, selling round flat bread—*lipioshka* in Russian or *non* in Tajik—from baby carriages and baskets.

Amidst these timeless people are the Russians and the modern Tajiks. In suits, or high heels or short skirts and no headscarves, they have the air of the future, walking beside their countrymen who are the past.

We reach the fortified gate to the United Nations compound too quickly. I want more time on the Tajik side of the heavily defended walls and forti-fied fences.

The armoured car lumbers to a stop, facing two layers of armed guards and a primary line of Tajik military at the gate to the compound. I open the door and step out of the armoured oven and enter through the gates, leav-ing Tajikistan behind, with a flash of my *laissez passer*, the UN passport. The guards touch their left hands to their breasts, bow slightly and shake hands with me.

I attend my first civil affairs section head meeting. I am the section head for the legal department. I have one person in my section, Suzanne, the Austrian lawyer. She does speak Russian, I come to learn, and is on her way out of the mission. I am to become the section head of a section with only a head.

The meeting is attended by the heads of Political, Information, Police, and Electoral sections—the standard non-military divisions in most United Nations missions. The chair of the meeting is our boss, Mr. Nagesh Bhatia, a former military officer in the Indian army. Army or former army personnel make up a large proportion of civilian staff working in the field.

The topic of this meeting is the recent murder of Otakhon Latifi, the op-position leader killed that very week. He was a journalist and senior opposi-tion leader. On September 22, 1998 he was shot dead as he left his home in Dushanbe. At the time of his death he was chair of the legal affairs committee of the National Reconciliation Commission, the joint government-opposition body charged with integrating the Islamic opposition into social and governmental structures in preparation for parliamentary elections. Most importantly, he was a key mediator, a moderate, and although allied with Tajikistan's former spiritual leader, Hoji Akbar Turajonzoda, he was opposed to political Islam and was closer to the secular wing of the opposition. Those responsible for the murder of Latifi had clearly wanted him dead to disrupt peace altogether. A compromiser is a threat to conflict, and to extremist ideology.

Bhatia is going around the room, asking each section head what they know about the murder and what, if anything, we are doing to find out who is responsible. He turns first to the political officer for insight into why Latifi was killed. He asks, "So what do you people think? Why have we lost this moderate man?"

A long silence follows the question. The political section is essential to a peacekeeping operation. Comprised of former diplomatic officials, from ambassadors to first secretaries, the job of the section is to keep informed of the current political situation and to carefully map out the possibilities for the future. This work requires staying well connected and well informed regarding where allegiances lie between and within the political players. It also requires an understanding of who holds actual power and of how stable the political environment is. In a country like Tajikistan, the political climate changes daily, as deals are made and unmade and participants are in—and then out of—favour. Information and solid sources of information are the key to this work. Contacts in government, business, non-governmental organizations, and even criminal organizations, must be used and checked daily to know what is happening. Once this information is gathered, it must be distilled and compared to known physical events, such as military actions, assassinations, open agreements, and alliances, in order to confirm what can be believed and what needs to be discarded. It is difficult and careful work. Trusting in the sources of information is important, but the sheer volume of contacts is equally important. Political officers must be active out in the community, constantly meeting, talking, asking questions. By nature they must be nosy and astute and subtle. Push hard and no one talks with you. Push too hard and you can end up dead.

Bhatia nods to the political officer who says, "These are dangerous times, Mr. Bhatia, it is best not to ask too many questions."

A slight shade of red begins to colour Bhatia's very prominent ears. "But, surely we have some information?" he asks.

The political officer nods, his head lowered. "Yes," he says, "our information is that we should be careful. The Garm killing. The killing of the SRGS's bodyguard last month. It is extremely dangerous to even pose questions here. We are too vulnerable."

I watch, with fascination, the deepening red of two very large ears. "Yes," Mr. Bhatia responds, "you are right, and you should know that I have recommended to the Security Council that we need an armed contingent of soldiers to continue with this peacekeeping work. This recommendation was turned down. So we sit here, unarmed, with a job to do. We must do it as well as we can and are able. Now, who have you talked to find out who and why Latifi was killed? What sources have we tried to gather?"

Heads are lowered around the room and Bhatia's cheeks and ears are now a uniform crimson.

"My cleaning lady," the political officer finally blurts out. "I have asked her."

"Your cleaning lady?" Bhatia replies. "What do you mean?"

"Yes," the political officer answers. "I mean the woman who cleans my room at the *dacha*. She tells me that we should not inquire into Latifi's death. It is too risky."

A silent embarrassment descends.

I will come to learn that our political analysts sit in the United Nations Headquarters, "the bunker," all day, reading news reports from wire services. They don't leave the bunker, except for official meetings and to return home. It occurs to me that we know nothing of what is happening beyond the layers of security guards that protect us from the country we are here to protect.

Team Garm is ambushed. De Marco is shot dead. Latifi, assassinated. All within two months. The Americans leave. Russia arms its fighter jets parked at Dushanbe airport. And we haven't a clue as to what is really going on.

YOU CAN'T LIVE THERE
(Dushanbe, Tajikistan—October 1998)

"Your apartment must have a steel outer door," the United Nations head of security is telling me. It is my security briefing three weeks after arriving in Tajikistan. "And must be within a security triangle, six blocks from this office." The UN office is a squat building beside the Ministry of Interior and across the street from the Ministry of Security, the former KGB. At the corner of the street is a statue of the founder of the Soviet KGB, Felix Dzerzhinsky. It is at once the safest and most dangerous place in Dushanbe.

He is showing me a blurred map of unnamed streets. A red marker has been drawn across the map in a triangle. Inside the triangle is the UN compound. Outside the triangle is the location of the apartment I have just rented.

The security chief points to it. "This is where you are now living. You can't live there. It is not safe. We cannot protect you there."

I have interacted with enough UN bureaucrats in my career to know that this one has no idea what he is talking about. He will receive his information only from local government sources and they will manipulate him for whatever interests they choose. In this case, perhaps, they own the apartments within the triangle and see an opportunity for excessive rents paid in American dollars. In a city in which the rent is $10 to $15 for an apartment, we will pay $200 to $500.

"The road that marks the boundary is here," he says, drawing his finger with authority over what appears to be a wide boulevard with a large memorial at its centre. I have walked by it enough times by now to know that it is a memorial to Second World War veterans. It is a full-sized tank, poised to roll over an enemy bunker.

"You live here," he says again, pointing to an area outside the triangle on the other side of the tank monument. "You can't live here."

"But I do live there," I say to him. "I don't see why twenty metres of road makes a difference for my security." It had taken me three weeks to find this apartment. It is cheap, has a hot water tank for showers, and is decorated in the traditional Tajik style, with rugs hanging on each wall. Most apartments I looked at were westernized and ugly: gleaming, clean, and expressionless. I liked the place I found. A Tajik opera singer owned it and was renting it to me.

"It has a steel door," I say to him.

He smiles a Cheshire grin and says, "Look. This street. The tank monument street. Last year two French citizens were kidnapped while walking along here. When the government arrested the kidnappers—well, they killed most of them—but the ones they arrested and interrogated said they chose this street because it was easy to use to drive from the city and into the countryside. That is the street you're telling me you want to live on?"

The security chief sees that I am unmoved by what he has told me. He may believe my insistence is naive bravado, but it is not. I simply do not trust anything he says to me.

Each morning, this security chief briefs the staff on the occurrences of the night before. For my first ten days in Tajikistan, I attended each and every one of these sessions and listened to the reports of the murders and mayhem of the night before.

"Where do you get the information you are briefing us on?" asked one of the veterans who has been on the mission for four years.

"Ministry of Interior," came the swift reply. In fact a Ministry of Interior officer lingered by the front door to the UN building. Our security chief and his crew went no further than the door for their information.

"Have you ever thought of speaking with the opposition side on security matters? They may have information also," the veteran said.

"No," responded the security officer curtly.

One morning after a night of bomb explosions and endless rifle fire, the security chief was asked what had been happening. He questioned the Ministry of Interior personnel stationed at our front door and then returned to say that nothing had actually occurred, that we were under too much stress and were hearing things going bump in the night.

Seeing my resolve to keep the apartment I had already found, the security chief uses his trump card. "Well," he says, rising up and out of his chair, knowing that he will succeed, "do as you wish. Remember, if something happens to you the UN will not be responsible. In any way." And so it goes. If I am injured or robbed or worse, the UN will not help. Medical bills will not be paid. Salary while I recuperate will be forfeited. I will be abandoned to make my way home to Canada on foot through the mountains and deserts of Central Asia and all because I lived on the wrong side of the red line on the Cheshire's map. He hit me where I was vulnerable: in the paycheque.

"You win," I say at last. "I'll move."

"Of course you will," he says. "Of course."

RADIO CHECK BEGINS IN ONE MINUTE
(Dushanbe, Tajikistan—October 1998)

I am alone in my apartment waiting for the red light on my radio to flicker
on. It is 9 p.m. The power is out in my flat, in my building, in the city.
Tajikistan neglected to pay its Uzbek cousin for gas this month. I forgot to
buy candles, so I sit in the dark, waiting.

My handset squawks, "Radio check begins in one minute." It is our security officer notifying us that check-in is about to start. At 9 p.m, we each
sit listening for our call sign, for our moment of human interaction over a
crackling bit of air. "Charlie Lima One, I read you loud and clear, over."
This will be my answer telling them I am alive, unharmed, and capable of
responding. I am neither skilled nor confident enough to respond with some
wit or military response. "I read you five by five," some would say, meaning
loud and clear. Very cool. One other, a Dane too long away from the little
mermaid in Copenhagen, a statue whose head kept getting lopped off for
sport, would offer a soliloquy of bad poetry or unfathomable wisdom on
most nights. Crazy, lonely stuff.

The security officer proceeds each night to radio to the staff members. On most nights I sit listening to everyone's call, then return to sitting in the dark wondering what the hell I am doing here.

It is late October and I have been in Tajikistan less than a month. A velvety rain sprinkles onto the city. The hard, dry clay resists becoming mud. It has been baked solid over a choking summer and fall and remains slippery and defiant until the heavy rain and snow begin. For now, the rain is only a relief from the monotony of clear skies and heat.

Outside, the rain. A familiar sound. I feel less lonely with it so close.

"Alpha Pappa One." The radio check begins. "Come in, over."

The radio checks began when De Marco died, I am told. The city is so quiet at night. Even the heavy thumps of machine guns going off at check points sound muted. No cars in the streets. No people. I long to see a tank groaning along.

I am on the fifth floor of my building. A wide, broken stairway that I stumble over each morning is my link to the outside. The first-floor tenants lock a steel ground-floor door to the stairway from the inside each night. There are bogeymen outside. They break down your wood doors and cut your head off to steal your watch.

"This is Alpha Pappa One. I read you loud and clear, over." My compatriot, the little Canadian chief administrative officer, crisply answers the call. Civil administration is big in the UN world. He is the day-to-day boss. The promotions boss. The reassignment to New York or Kosovo boss. He is licked dry by packs of career-stalled, desperate prunes every day. He is a physically small man who smokes big cigars and listens to prunes who call him boss.

He is the one who ordered radio check each night. He lives in a fortified compound called the *dacha*. He is guarded by soldiers. He eats imported cheese and smokes his cigars and drinks whisky. The rest of us are in the city, waiting for our heads to be cut off.

"Alpha Sierra, come in, over."

How will I survive here?

Don't answer your door to anyone.

Don't keep your window open.

Don't go out at night.

Don't display wealth.

Don't bring locals into your apartment.

Don't eat meat on Fridays.

Many of the UN soldiers are living with a prostitute-girlfriend. The little Canadian Napoleon who was the head of civil administration told me when I arrived: "Listen," he said, "stay away from the local women. They are beautiful. You risk your job. And your life. Stay away from sex." He lingered over the word "sex" so that it came out as sexsssss. I think he may also have drooled a little.

Long-legged Russians, Persians with beautiful bodies, big toes and teeth, bad skin and wild hair. "Ronald," one such woman said to me. "Teach me English and I will teach you to dance." I smiled and clicked my heels together. It was a stupid reflex that I just then developed. Regrettably, she noticed, looked at my feet and pointed. "Ha, ha," she said, and then in polite imitation she clicked her heels together. "Canada?" She asked and pointed.

"Yes," I said in deep embarrassment, "Canada."

I pace the floor, radio in hand, then step out onto my balcony, breaking the rules. The fresh air feels good and this act of daring lifts my spirits. "You are being watched. Followed," we are told. "If they find where you live, they will break in. You are rich, for them, and make an easy target." I hear the warnings from our security briefing and stay against the wall on the balcony, in the shadows.

"Charlie Lima One," I hear my radio sign. Civil legal advisor for the mission. "Come in, over." Someone is thinking about me.

"I read you loud and clear, over," I say. My moment has come and gone. I am alone again. My thoughts turn to Canada, and to Antonia, the woman I have left behind.

I met Antonia in Toronto practising law in a hive of lawyers barely sustaining livelihoods in an enormous struggle against the government of Canada over rights for non-citizens. I rented space with that crew and started my practice as an immigration lawyer. We worked hard, were often paid with scrunched up balls of money, Toys R Us certificates, melons, and anything else our near destitute clients could muster. Once, I was paid with a box of meat.

Antonia and I often worked late into the night. Drinks, food, dance, and sex followed. We closed down the Devil's Martini many a night.

I had worked and lived for years with the United Nations in various postings in Asia and so had become accustomed to a life of serial monogamy. I changed partners when I changed geography so, when I decided to leave Toronto for Tajikistan in 1998 I knew I was moving on and that I might not see Antonia again. This was all new to her, I imagined, and so when I said my goodbye at the airport, I took her aside and away from friends who had gathered for the farewell.

"Toni," I said, my eyes brimming. "I have to go now, my plane's been called."

"Goodbye," she said, her eyes dry and focused.

"I will call. I will write."

"Good," she said, looking back at our friends.

"I don't think you understand," I finally said.

She turned her head to me. "Of course I do," she said. "You're going to Tajikistan. We may never see each other again. But maybe we will. No promises, or commitments. Steady heart." She kissed me hard and walked away. The memory of that goodbye, of her confidence and independence, would keep me enthralled and thinking only of her and calling Canada from satellite phones and sending her e-mails that bounced through New York from Tajikistan. I vowed that I would find a way to stay in some form of contact with this Hungarian/ Pole who smoked too much, worked too hard, and looked a lot like Rita Hayworth.

I hear noises in the hallway, outside the door of my Dushanbe apartment. Muffled sounds. I tense and move inside, radio ready. Then—a pounding on my door. My heart races. I recall the words of the security officer: "Don't answer the door. Call security." The door reverberates again. Pound, pound, pound. Is it friendly? I wait, sweating, holding my breath.

A Polish political officer with lengthy experience in Tajikistan told me a story. A knock came on his door one night. He opened it to face a pistol. The pistol holder entered. They spoke Russian together. The man was looking for another, to kill, he said. Was he here? "No," said the Pole. "Not here. Come in and take a drink with me." The would be murderer was already drunk. They sat over a bottle.

"The man takes his boots off. The stench from his feet made me sick for a week," the political officer told me. "All I really remember after the pistol are the feet," he said.

As I stand completely still in my apartment listening for the clang of tools pulling down my door, all I can think of are those feet. I am hesitant to call our security people. I have been critical of our paranoia and our distance from the locals and am already known for this. I am told repeatedly that I do not understand the Tajiks, that they are a different people, a lazy, violent, unpredictable people who cannot be trusted. They are not worth knowing, I am told, and it is dangerous to know them. I can't now cry wolf until I see teeth.

I am afraid, standing alone in the dark, straining to hear voices outside.

A long silence. They're gone, I think.

Then. "Excuse me, sir," an English voice calls from behind the door. "Please, we are your neighbours. Downstairs. Hello!"

Is this some trick? I ask myself.

"Please, sir," the voice says again. The use of *sir* gets me. I rush to the door and pull back the heavy metal bolts and slowly push it open. I see a man in pyjamas standing with his arms folded looking angry. Pyjamas! I open the door fully to see a younger man standing nearby. The young man speaks, "Sir, water from you is coming to us." He smiles and gestures at the ceiling, then floor. Seeing my confusion, he says, "Bath. Bath. When you bath. Water comes to us.... Please. Stop...." Pyjamas looks sternly at me.

"Sorry," I say. "I will speak to the owner. "

They both nod. Pyjamas looks very angry.

As the men turn to head down the stairs, the younger man looks back at me and smiles. "Every night we are scared," he says. "It is normal in Dushanbe." My face and hesitations have told them everything and they have responded with compassion and empathy.

My fear now gone, I only feel warmth as I watch my neighbours make their careful way down the stairs.

LONG-LEGGED DICTIONARY

(Fan Mountains, Tajikistan—November 1998)

At a checkpoint, a pimple-faced Russian soldier peers into the taxi that is taking me out of the city. He is young and blushes easily as our driver jokes with him. He doesn't say a word. His face is an inch or less from the driver's open window and, as he leans in, I see the hammer-and-sickle medallion on his fur hat. A remnant of a fallen empire. The driver continues to talk to him. It is a critical moment at the checkpoint and I try to look relaxed. We are driving north from Dushanbe towards Leninobod on a mountain road that is laced with police and army checkpoints. At the Tajik police barriers that we must make our way through, our driver tries a quick wave and smile. If the police flinch he stops immediately and quickly jumps out. I watch him embrace each policeman at the barriers. Some he will kiss. Each time, he finds one to walk to the side of the road with and shake hands. Money passes and we are away.

The army is different. In the open road they are watchful, alert. They will take their share of bounty, but not this way. They stop trucks and buses and take their time. A lone car, however, is only a potential threat.

The young soldier regards me with interest. Our driver's chatter is non-stop. He is searching for whatever it is this soldier needs to hear.

Suddenly, Tomasz, the Polish military officer in the back seat, lets out a burst of laughter.

"He is clever, our driver," says Tomasz in English. "He says you are journalist and that if we are delayed further you will take the boy's picture. A journalist for CNN has more power here than a lawyer for the United Nations, dear friend." The Pole smiles broadly at the soldier and speaks to him in Russian. The boy's blush deepens.

I have been in Tajikistan over one month doing little more than reading reports and being told to be afraid. It is time, I have decided, to breach our security regulations and leave Dushanbe in a private car. I need to see more of Tajikistan than the six square blocks of the city centre and the wall-sized map on our briefing room. It is time to stretch my legs in this country and to end my isolation.

The Russians man the roads to ensure that the drug trade proceeds unimpeded. By 1998, 30,000 Russian troops had settled along the Tajik-Afghan border, waiting. Keeping the peace. Keeping out the *mujaheds*. Waiting for something to happen. To ease the tedium and make money, they run a drug trade. The most heavily armed drug traffickers in the world. So the roads have to be kept reasonably safe to keep the drugs moving to their markets.

"I have confirmed it to him," says the Pole. "You are journalist. Smile to him and we will be permitted through." I smile and the boy steps back from the car and waves, but not to us. An officer strolls to the car, Kalashnikov slung over one shoulder. He is a short, balding man with a face like gravel. He is smiling. We have the conversation again. This time the officer nods and asks questions. *He* is telling the jokes and our driver and the Pole laugh. The Pole translates. "You are taking a risk to go on this road, says the officer. Please, go back. He finds it funny, what we are doing. He is polite, however." The Pole talks and the officer laughs, looking right at me.

The Lada slips into gear and the driver smiles. He has a gold incisor and it gleams at me as he turns and nods. "Good," is all he can say. Wrapping his *chapan* coat tightly around him, the driver momentarily takes both hands from the wheel, then shifts gears and sends the Russian car careening down the road.

I turn to the Pole. "What did you tell him?" I ask.

"Nothing," he says. "Only that you are virgin." He says this seriously, without laughter.

"What?"

"I said to him that you are virgin and that we are trying to help you find girl." He stares at me until he can no longer restrain himself, then laughs out loud and with gusto. Slapping my shoulder, he says, "Don't worry, a different officer will be on duty when we return tonight."

"Thank you, Tomasz," I say.

"You are welcome," he says and laughs again.

Tomasz is a Polish captain at the end of his tour of duty in the country. It is his first peacekeeping assignment and he has loved it. While other UN soldiers huddled in the bunker of the UN compound drinking too much Tiger beer, cursing the tedium, and planning their next monthly holiday, Tomasz has spent most of his time out with the people of Tajikistan. He made friends, improved his Russian, explored the mountains, found the best places to eat, and fell heavily, inexorably in love. His Tajik girlfriend, Afsana, sits with him now in the back seat.

I had asked him once, as he sat telling of the virtues of multiple language skills, to teach me Russian. He declined. "There is only one way to learn," he said. "You require a long-legged dictionary. There are many. Choose one."

At last through the checkpoint, we are on our way into the mountains in a long, slow climb on a slice of road that hangs like a window washer's trestle on the mountain side. Red and grey rocks rise straight up on our right side. On the left, centimetres from where our tire clings to the road, the drop is sheer. We stop for a look and get out of the car. The driver points to a section of the slope halfway down. "Car," he says. I finally see it, the twisted ball of metal that has few characteristics of a car left. I notice a tire in the mangle. "One week ago," our driver says. He shakes his head and unwraps and wraps his *chapan* coat. The car has fallen from the spot we are standing on. I think I find the depression at the road's edge where the wheel lost its grip. Our driver sees it also and bends to pile a small monument of rocks. I lower my head in homage to the moment but Tomasz sees my sombre gesture and says, "He is marking danger, not saying a prayer. He drives road often and must know the weaknesses. Also alert others, I suppose. You see," he points along the edge of road to similar cairns of rock. "Others have done the same."

I count three other piles within a hundred metres. From the location of each pile, I trace a line down the cliff face until I find another vehicle pinned against a jutting outcrop of bolder. They are red with rust and completely flattened from the fall.

Team Garm's car fell from a road just like the one we are on. When it stopped rolling the doors were sealed shut and the chassis compressed to half its size. The only way to reach the car was by helicopter. Oddly, the four bodies were not found in the car but strewn across the cliff face. One was found in a tree. It is one of the lingering mysteries of the killing.

"This road is dangerous," I say to Tomasz.

He is standing beside me, looking at the wrecks.

"They were careless," he says as he pulls at the corner of his cropped moustache. "The road is good. Our driver is good. The car … works. It's enough for me." He surveys me, eyebrow arched and mischievous. "You?" he asks.

I follow the road on its slow ascent up the mountain. A few other cars and lorries creep along it, disappearing on the long bends that wrap around bulges in the mountainside. When they re-emerge into view, the road has climbed considerably and they are insects on the torso of this great monster. I feel suddenly small and cold.

I look out over the vastness of space that fills the gap between the dozen or so mountain peaks surrounding us. Each peak has permanent snow—the grey hair of these giants that have watched over Tajikistan for centuries. They have watched dinosaurs flourish, then die away, Alexander the Great strutting impatiently, and the Bolsheviks arriving. Over the barren slopes dotted with scraggly bushes and a barber's brush cut worth of grass, they have felt the "Great Game" players of England and Russia pass, searching, ever searching for a way to the promised land, India, and finding instead the dungeons of Buchara and an emir's sharp impatience.

I have never seen such vast, empty space. A lone bird hangs in the air, wings outstretched. It effortlessly rides the currents, up, then down.

I turn to Tomasz. "Please, let's continue. But tell the driver to drive slowly."

Tomasz wrinkles his already wrinkled face and laughs. "Of course," he says.

His face is red from the cold; we walk to the car.

I peer over the edge of road and down at the wrecks on the mountainside below. One last look. I wonder if the bodies are still trapped inside.

I watch our driver's concentration as he pulls at the metre-long gearshift located on his right side. Brow deeply furrowed, he has extended his lower lip to wrap around the bottom portion of his moustache. As he changes gears and pushes the shift down to second gear, he sucks furiously on the moustache. The car is climbing onto a narrowing of the road. A sharp curve lies ahead and it is not possible to see around it for oncoming vehicles. Beside us is a sheer drop of 1000 metres. Open the door and step into the sky.

The car is travelling as fast as our driver can push it. I can see the frustration in his face now, as he tries to gain more speed but cannot. At first I think him demonic for such recklessness but then I realize what he is doing. I hear the sound of another vehicle. It is travelling towards us and is on the other side of the bend, out of view. Our driver has heard it also and wants to be at the bend first, as only one vehicle at a time can pass. His foot holds the gas pedal to the floor and the engine groans. The road seems to crest and then momentarily flatten. He shifts hard and we are travelling faster. I close my eyes. I can hear the other vehicle, closer now, but just out of view. If we both enter the corner together, we will collide. There is no place to go but into the other car, or over the cliff.

I open my eyes as we begin the turn. Small rocks by the road's edge are sent flying down the cliff face by our tires and as we enter the curve at high speed the car fishtails slightly and it feels, for a moment, as if the rear left tire is treading only on air. Even Tomasz is concerned. He speaks to the driver in Russian and he laughs and replies.

"I have told him he is driving too fast," Tomasz says.

"Good. He is. What did he say?" The car has not slowed.

"He says there are no sheep on the road."

"What does that mean?" I ask.

"It means there is no sheep on the road and, I suppose, he will keep driving as he is driving," Tomasz answers.

We have won the corner. As we come around to the other side, our driver smiles and nods. A lone car idles a distance from the turn, waiting for us to pass.

Tomasz shakes his head and laughs. "Tajiks," he says knowingly. "A big risk for a little road."

A cloud of dust rises up behind our car and, through the prayer beads hanging on the front mirror and over and past the front hood, I see only sky. I sit back in the cracked and ripped leather bucket seat and resign myself to the ride. *Inshallah*, I say to myself, God willing.

We are on the back of the dragon—rows of peaks that rise to points and then down again to valleys. In the valleys, even at this altitude of barrenness, villages cling. A few scattered mud, straw, and dung huts are attached to the mountainside. Steep trails lead up from the road to the huts. It is a relief to see the homes, to be off the precipice and to be slowing down to stop.

Small children are sitting on their haunches by the roadside, watching us with wide eyes. They have stopped their games for us and have eased down to a squat, a familiar position in the mountains of this country. As we uncurl ourselves from the confines of the Lada, a boy appears on the road leading what seems to be a prickly quilled donkey. As the donkey nears we can see that two bunches of dry sticks are draped over its back, concealing both flanks. The boy turns to us without saying a word and keeps his eyes on us as we pass. We say hello and he ignores us. Afsana, the woman with us, offers the children chocolate. They ask her what it is. They have never seen it before, she tells me.

A man emerges from one of the huts and approaches us. He and our driver shake hands, careful to use the right hand, their left flat against the chest. We are invited for lunch.

We are feted with plates overflowing with fresh lamb and pilaf. For days I have been eating cheese and bread and spaghetti behind the steel door of my apartment and so I devour this fresh meat. Our Tajik hosts smile at my obvious relish. Between the courses of meat I ask, through Tomasz, how they survive in winter. The men tell me that in one month the road we are on will close because of snow and that they will be cut off from the outside world. Bread and rice and stored meats, they say, and God's grace will sustain them. God's grace was delivered by Soviet helicopters in the past, I know. Some Russian helicopters remain, but these days they are loaded only with armaments.

I inquire into a curiosity that I have harboured since being assigned to Tajikistan. The Central Asians play a game on horseback involving the carcass of what I believe to be a sheep. It is a violent, aggressive game. In order to score or win the contest, a rider must cross a finish line while struggling to hold onto the carcass as the other riders, sometimes in the hundreds, lash him and collide with him and grab at him. I know of the game because of a film, *The Horsemen*, with Omar Sharif, which I saw many years ago. I also know of it from a Turkmen friend in Canada who had urged me to find the game while I was in the region. "It will change your perspective of Central Asia," he said to me. "Whatever has happened in the present, this game will take you to their past."

I describe the sport to Tomasz and he is mystified. He has been in the country for a year and has never heard of such an event. He translates what I have described to our hosts. They lean forward, listening intently. After Tomasz finishes they look from one to another and then at me. Then they laugh. Great, hearty, warlike laughter.

"Thank you, Ron," says Tomasz sarcastically.

"I thought it was Central Asia," I say.

"Wait...." Tomasz says. The men speak to him and he nods. They laugh again.

"I see," says Tomasz. "It is not a sheep. It is a headless goat. They laugh at you because you said sheep."

The men then explain to us that the game is rarely played now because of the fighting. They have not seen a game in years. I am disappointed by this news. A sheep! they say, and laugh again.

The meal finishes and the Tajik men pass open palms lightly over their faces, forehead to chin. It is the Muslim custom after meals, our driver tells us. As we walk back to the car, our driver says to Tomasz that he is a player of the game I seek, that it is called buzkashi and that he himself will be in a large game in a few weeks just outside Dushanbe.

I ask Tomasz, "How can we find it?"

He relays the question and replies, "Just follow the horses...."

"Why didn't he mention this game when I asked the village men about it?" I ask Tomasz.

He answers with what is his standard response, and a response I will hear often from UN personnel in the country. "He is Tajik," says Tomasz with a snort of laughter. "Who knows?"

Two more hours of driving to reach Ayni, the highest point on this mountain range. Here we stop for tea and a brief trek into the mountains. A manned weather station sits atop the Ayni peak. From here, over 3000 metres above sea level, the road roller-coasters downward to Leninobod (renamed Sughd in 2000) the northern province of Tajikistan. In November 1998, three weeks after the day I stand at Ayni, this province will be invaded from Uzbekistan by Tajik exiles. They will come in force with tanks and truckloads of soldiers. They will take the airport and enter the city and proclaim secession of the north. The furthest point this invading army will travel south will be here, at Ayni, where government troops coming from the south will battle their way through—or so we are later told.

We, the international community, are told so much in Tajikistan by the government. We are given figures for demobilized government soldiers and figures of opposition fighters in so-called assembly or cantonment areas. We are told that crime is under control in Dushanbe, that the police are taking active measures to ensure it continues to decline, and that the judicial system lacks resources but is doing a pretty fair job, all things considered. We are told about everyone's commitment to peace through democracy, and how this year a lasting peace will be achieved. We are told that free speech is sacrosanct. The government tells us that the opposition consists of Islamic fundamentalists determined to build an Islamic state. The opposition tells us that the government continues to be communist and that they are criminals and undemocratic.

We believe everything we hear. Everything we are told has some truth in it, I am sure. But most of it is crafted to feed into the needs of the international community. The embassies need to report that peace is close, so that their capitals see them as being in an important place. The UN needs to tell the embassies that peace is close so that donations for peacekeeping continue. The government tells us that the opposition is Islamic fundamentalist because they know the US hates fundamentalists and will more likely back the government with money. The opposition believes the US hates communists more, and that, although the US will not side with Islam, they may at least stay neutral. Dushanbe must be perceived as safe, so the government is seen to be in control. Both opposition and government need the international community to believe that they are committed to democratic principles to ensure World Bank and other funding.

I listen to what the government reports and I listen to us, the UN, and the international community, reporting as though it were true.

As I stand now at Ayni peak, a stiff cold wind howling and whistling through the boulders around me, I look out over this jagged country and listen to a faint voice rising up from the valley.

"Off with his head!" says the voice. "Off with his head!"

A VERY DIFFERENT LIFE

(Fan Mountains, Tajikistan—November 1998)

There may be moments in UN operations in which the diplomatic corps and the bureaucrats in New York and the field staff have a cold, careful eye trained on the realities of a country. They know the players so well that any political or military gambit is understood well before it occurs, and steps are taken by the international community to forestall disaster or encourage compromise. Military is brought up, private dialogue held, promises made, threats made. In the end, a crisis averted with skill, tact, and planning. Unfortunately, I have never seen a UN operation handled in such a manner. They seem doomed to chance. A peacekeeping mission is either peopled by outsiders who deal in superficial or academic understandings of the country they occupy, or peopled by nationalities too close to what is happening to remain impartial and unbiased. In either case, any kind of effective and neutral negotiations, resource allocation, and setting of priorities is often muddled by a lack of knowledge or, worse, by an agenda. Success may still occur and elections held (the panacea of all UN operations—elections!) but not because UN personnel in the field brilliantly orchestrated the success. Success in peacekeeping is more often due to a confluence of coincidence, good fortune, and fatigue on the part of enemies.

Two camps existed within the UN enclave in Tajikistan. Those from the world community who spoke none of the local languages were largely from the West, including Canada, and were dutiful, conscientious, and obedient. They stayed in the UN compound, except to travel home to their steel-doored apartments. They obeyed curfew, answered radio checks, and never ventured beyond the limits of Dushanbe into the rows of mountains that filled every window frame of every apartment in the city. They relied on alcohol, pirated videos of old British TV shows, and the creeping onset of their own insanity as sources of entertainment. Alone in their apartments as their steel doors clanged shut, they would sit, safe, often by candlelight as the electricity failed. Nothing to read. Nothing to watch. No one to talk to except for the once-a-night crackle of a radio security check.

I quickly came to learn, however, that a second camp of staff members led a very different life in Dushanbe. They were composed largely of Poles, who spoke Russian, and an assortment of other Russian speakers. They came without illusions, to earn a handsome United Nations pay in Tajikistan, to save some money, and to stay alive. For this group of men, the staying alive part meant keeping the body as well as the soul alive. They liberally explored the countryside, befriended locals, had girlfriends, went out to restaurants after curfew, and killed time by living outside the fortress United Nations and so ensured that the insidious onset of time would not kill them. They travelled outside of the security zone of the city centre, took trains and horses and local airlines. From the moment I arrived in the country, I knew that I wanted to befriend these men and to learn something more of Tajikistan than the number of fighters in each faction, the progress of the constitutional debate, and the mood of stakeholders, regional governments who needed peace and stability in Tajikistan. The overlying purpose of my work for the UN would remain the same, but the value of my ability to contribute would grow with knowledge of the culture, if I dared to step outside our security boundary. It would also be a lot more fun. Tomasz was of this camp.

I met Tomasz in September 1998 while travelling into Tajikistan through Uzbekistan and Kazakhstan. He was returning from leave in Uzbekistan and was anxious to return to his Central Asian home, to Tajikistan. He considered it home and at one point in his tour had inquired into becoming a Tajik citizen. Such was his commitment to the country. His wife and children in Poland awaited his return and wondered why he had delayed so long.

The reason lies huddled against the cold of Ayni in the back seat of the taxi we hired to drive us out of the gates of Dushanbe and into the mountains. Afsana, his girlfriend, is ethnic Russian and living in Tajikistan. Tomasz fell hard for her and she wanted him to take her with him back to Poland. The question has been posed again on our car trip, and, an answer not forthcoming, she huddles in the back seat, refusing to get out.

"She wants me not to stay," Tomasz says to me. "But to take her to Poland. Give her an apartment."

"And your wife?" I ask.

He frowns and wrinkles his forehead so that he looks like an old dog with loose folding skin. "My wife would not be happy. But, Afsana does not care if I keep my wife. She wants to be with me in Poland. So, maybe I take her." He looks at me with his dog's face. "What do you think, Ronald?"

I see the disaster unfolding, see her returning to Poland with him, knowing no one but Tomasz, being cut off from family, language, culture, wanting him, his time, becoming jealous for it. Tragedy looms in that idea.

"Sounds fine," I say. "Great idea."

He eyes me with one arching eyebrow, then laughs. "It is stupid idea, no?"

I nod. "Oh, yes," I say. "Very stupid."

I have witnessed soldiers leaving embattled countries with new wives or girlfriends in tow. It happened often. Peacekeeping operations or wars brought in soldiers who lived meagre if not borderline lives in their home countries and became intoxicated with their relative power and wealth in the countries in which they served. With money to spend, nice vehicles to drive, and the myth that everyone lived in luxury in the West, a soldier could win a stunning local beauty, and sweep her away. Or worse, he could stay.

I turn to Tomasz on the Ayni summit and look at him. I will tell him to forget Afsana, to go back to Poland, care for his wife, his sons, and forget this place that will be no more than a dream as he settles back into a Poland Airways flight from Uzbekistan when he leaves in a few weeks. He will close his eyes and the war, the peace, the generals, the cold, the fears he lived with here, will vanish: just another conflict in another distant part of the world, and he has to get the kids to school on time anyway, no time to think about another country's problems. I will tell him this, to leave his long-legged dictionary in Tajikistan, where he found her.

Tomasz is now making faces at the car, and walking in an elaborate duck's waddle to elicit a laugh from inside, from the bundle in the back seat. It seems to be working. She begins laughing and calling him stupid.

"She calls me stupid," he says to me, face alight with a smile.

He finally stops his waddle and turns to me. "So, Ronald, tell me what to do."

The wind gusts at that moment and I feel the chill of winter approaching. With the snow the pass will close, the narrow mountain road become impassable and the mountain people cut off. They scramble now to store enough food to last the winter's isolation. Some will certainly die over winter, and when helicopters can fly, which they rarely do amidst the gusts of frozen air in these mountains, supplies will be brought in—sometimes doctors. For now, the mountain people brace themselves for the long struggle to stay alive.

After a pause I turn to Tomasz and say, "I can't tell you what to do. You love her. You love your wife and children. You created this. You decide it. It gives me a headache."

He looks at me with his dog's forehead and laughs until the entire valley seems to be echoing with that laugh. He then completely ignores what I have said, as, I come to learn, is his custom.

"The problem for Tajiks lies in geography," he suddenly says to me. Closing his hands into a fist. "It is false country, squeezed into shape by neighbours. It should not exist, really." A map of Tajikistan reflects Tomasz's viewpoint. The centre of the country is depressed at its edges, and bulges slightly at either end, like some giant had gripped the country in an open palm, then slowly squeezed it into a misshapen hourglass.

"Tajiks have no sense of who they are," he continues. "So they ... Ronald, what is a word for to ... drift."

"Drift is a good word," I say. "Or flounder."

"Yes, flounder. I like that word. The Tajiks flounder. That explains why they are crazy. The borders of these countries make no sense. None. No one respects them. Except the Russians. The Russians made them. When your country makes no sense and you flounder, you go mad. The Tajiks are mad."

Tomasz pulls at the end of his half-inch, jet-black moustache that sits below his nose like a fuzzy caterpillar and reminds me of Charlie Chaplin's moustache, or maybe Hitler's. I tell Tomasz this.

"Hitler...!" He shrieks, then bursts out laughing. "Paw, you are funny, funny man, Ronald." He arches his eyebrow and his face darkens. "How have you stayed alive?"

We start to walk back to the car. "At least," he says, "you don't have donkey sense to tell me who to love. Or, where to love."

With that, my captain who is part poet and all romantic and I climb back into the rusting Lada for the long and treacherous trip back to Dushanbe from Ayni summit. As he wedges himself into the back seat, Tomasz put his face to within an inch of Afsana's and blows kisses at her until her pretense of anger melts into a fit of giggles and laughter and into the warmth of their cuddling.

ALWAYS AN OUTSIDER

(Ayni, Tajikistan—November 1998)

To the mountain clans, the United Nations observation teams scattered into the mountains in 1998 were never more than outsiders. They could have been Russian military or UN, it didn't matter a great deal. Westerners would always be outsiders. If a clan leader directed that these outsiders should die, then no question was asked: the order would be acted on.

So it was that the outsiders of Team Garm were in trouble, and they knew it. On June 15, 1998, six weeks before being ambushed and killed, UN political officer Akino filed a briefing report of a meeting he attended with opposition field commanders in the Garm region. In his report he stated that one of the field commanders, from Komsomolobad, suggested that the safety of UN personnel was no longer guaranteed. Akino also noted that the Tajik field commander appeared visibly angry at the presence of UN personnel at the meeting and treated the team as a potential enemy.

On July 17, 1998, three days before the ambush, military observer Szewczk of Team Garm wrote a report in which he related the content of a discussion he had had with United Tajik Opposition Field Commander Sirojiddoin, (a.k.a. Sairridin) from an assembly area in Navabad, again within the Garm region. He stated that the field commander "is really fed up with UNMOT, the government and the UTO. His 250 soldiers' blood is boiling with anger and hate. They perhaps will kill UNMOT people even tomorrow, nobody can stop them." He added further that "if UNMOT HQ do not clarify urgently the matter of supplying foods and bedding stuffs to Sangi Malik UNMOT personnel may be endangered under the circumstances."

As our driver retraces our route down the slice of road away from Ayni and gathers speed, I reflect on the reports of the promises and betrayals and of the warnings to the men of Team Garm. They must have feared the worst, based on the cables they had sent. But did they ever believe the ambush was truly possible?

I turn to Tomasz. "Have you been to Garm?" I ask him.

"Garm. Yes, yes, of course I have. Why?" The mere mention of this name elicits a reaction. He sits up, looks seriously at me.

"Is it like this, I mean the road? Is the road like this one, so narrow and ... dangerous?"

"Of course," responds Tomasz, looking out the side window and toward the ledge, now to our right as we descend.

The road is wide enough for two cars or a truck and car to pass. It is a tight squeeze, but possible.

"So, why did they stop? I mean Garm. Why did they stop their car?"

The preliminary report I have from the prosecutor is that the Garm vehicle left their team site at 9:35, the morning of July 20, 1998. At 10:30 a.m. they crossed a government military checkpoint at a place called Labi Jar on the way to a meeting at Blue Lake with opposition field commander Mirzo Ziyoev. By 1:15 p.m. Garm was on the move back to its team site. It recrossed the Labi Jar checkpoint. At some point between Labi Jar and their team site, Garm was met and stopped by a second vehicle, a red Nissan being driven in the opposite direction. The occupants of the Nissan purportedly told the UN members that Mirzo Ziyoev wanted them to return to Blue Lake for further discussions. They then turned around and led the Nissan back to Blue Lake and to Mirzo Ziyoev. Along the road, the Nissan, following the UN vehicle, flashed its lights at them to stop. The UN vehicle stopped and the driver got out. As he approached the Nissan he was shot.

Those remaining in the vehicle, unarmed and defenceless, were then shot where they sat.

Given the tension in the region, I am puzzled by why Team Garm would risk stopping for the Nissan. I query Tomasz about this.

He thinks for a moment. "I don't know. They knew them, trusted them, had no choice, I don't know."

"But that is my problem, Tomasz. They were stopped the first time, according to the prosecutor, and told to return to Blue Lake. They didn't think that odd?"

"Maybe they did."

"But no radio call to their camp, to the operator on standby reporting this event? They were going to be late in returning because they now were heading back to Blue Lake, but they didn't report this?"

"All right, so what are you saying? That they were not returning to Blue Lake?"

Our driver is slowing the car at a bend in the road. A truck sits immobile on the road at the turn. We pull up behind it. Mumbling quickly, our driver leaves our car and walks to the truck.

"It is broken down," says Tomasz. "He will offer them help. It is the way of this road, to help each other."

"Is that what Garm did? Were they getting out to help someone in the road?"

Tomasz thinks for a moment and then says, "So what? They are dead. They were ambushed, either by blinking lights and having our men stop, or by broken car trick. Why matters? They are dead."

He is right, of course, it doesn't seem to really matter what actually happened. Where it counts to me, however, is in gauging the prosecution and police account. It renders their report untrustworthy.

Between the blinding refractions of sunlight that splay out through a windscreen mottled with dirt and dead insects, I watch our driver in deep conversation with the truck men. The seriousness of their expressions makes me uneasy, as our driver repeatedly points back to his Lada and to the fat, flush, UN types inside. The road is empty now and dusk is approaching, a dangerous time to be on this slice of road. The thought crosses my mind that we are being set up, that men with Russian-made AK-47s will bound down from the truck and spray our car with bullets. We are sitting ducks here. The UN briefings on security come to mind.

Each morning was the same at UNHQ in Dushanbe. Soldiers, each in their separate country khaki, with a blue UN patch on the shoulder, sat in rigid rows beside the civilian staff in suits, or coats, cold in the under-heated room. An officer stood in front of us and a wall-sized map with red and black markings on it, telling us what had happened the night before.

"Last night at eleven hundred hours, a Russian pensioner was attacked and killed inside her apartment. Her blood was used to write the words 'go home' on her walls." The officer's story referred to a common occurrence. The ethnic Russians who could not afford to leave Tajikistan once the war started were easy targets for the extremists, and for the criminals. Despite the presence of the Russian military, or perhaps because of it, the few remaining Russian civilians lived on the edge of poverty, fear, and neglect. They were attacked in the street. Their homes were taken. They were murdered. Resentment towards Russians was an historical feature of life, from as early as the Bolsheviks, and it fuelled and radicalized fundamentalists' fervour. It was a terrible circumstance, this vulnerability, regardless of what past wrongs may have been done.

The reality of being Russian in Tajikistan in November of 1998 was driven home to me one morning as I walked to work along the tree-lined boulevard of Rudaki. The sun was strong and despite the progress of fall to winter I felt hot amidst the swirls of wind-gusted leaves. Snow had already capped the mountains surrounding us. I was carrying my jacket in one arm and I felt happy, a happiness that came from having cold bones warmed by the sun. I had paused to point my face skyward to relish the heat, when I heard a clanging, crunching grind of wounded metal coming down the road. The toxic smell of something black was on me and I turned to watch a tank slowly pushing its way forward in the posture of a large, proud iron duck, beak held high. A soldier's torso extended out from inside a well at the top. He gripped a 50-calibre machine gun, pointing it to the side, in my general direction. I stepped back from the street. Other soldiers were sitting on the outer hull of the tank, on a flat portion at the sides and back, holding rifles, the ubiquitous AK-47. They were watching for something.

What came behind the tank explained their alertness. Although I did not fully realize it until later, this tank and these men were escorts. As it passed me, I saw a small green and black bus following within a foot or two of the tank's back track. Inside the bus a soldier sat driving, and his passengers, their own faces stern like the grown-ups', were children, a dozen or more, ranging in age from seven to fourteen. On their way to school that morning, these children of Russian officers were under the protective escort of a tank. I came to learn that in the savagery of this war and after-war, the Russian children had become direct targets, just as the Tajik children had been burned and strafed in the mountains years earlier by the Russians. A child for a child. One caught my eye as the bus inched past, always staying close to the shadow of the tank. He was a small boy with very white skin and big ears. His cheeks were pink. The Caucasian complexion was unmistakable in this land of olive skin. He looked at me and neither smiled nor mouthed any word to me. His face was impassive.

These memories are interrupted by the officer's droll voice. "This morning two decapitated heads were found on the tank monument near the KGB headquarters. They have not been identified."

"Yesterday afternoon, Rahmon Hitler's group fought Mohamed Ali's here, two kilometres from the city." He pointed to a spot on the map. "This territory," he said, drawing a circle around a small area on the map, "is claimed by both. They fired rocket grenades and used anti-tank weapons at each other. We have no word of casualties." As I lay in bed the night before I had heard the sounds of distant explosions, the sounds of this fight. The opposition faction in the war was a compilation of many different bands of fighters and of leaders. They held a tenuous loyalty to the UTO leadership but in the grey days of after-war, they were jockeying for survival, for land, and for control of areas of roads from which they could collect tolls and road tax, their main source of income. Clashes over the more favourable areas of road were common, something the government police and military couldn't control. They were too weak.

The briefing continues with these and similar reports and then with the usual caution. "Military are reminded to alternate their attire, not to wear their uniform each day, for security reasons. Further, for everyone, please use an alternative route to work each day. This decreases the risk of kidnapping. Thank you."

Infused with a morning's cup of Nescafé coffee that tasted like poison and a hearty dollop of fear, we in the United Nations begin our day.

As I watch our driver gesticulate and point and plan our murder, Tomasz sees the uncertain look on my face. He loses no time in making fun of me.

"Ronald, he is a good man. He is a taxi driver, not a suicide bomber. We are safe here."

"I know that," I answer defensively.

"Good," he says, "now go back to being detective."

"Nothing else, I just found that odd … the way they say it happened. That Garm stopped twice for that car, that's all. They would have seen the first time that the men were armed, and probably anxious about what they had been ordered to do. I just don't see an experienced team like Garm stopping again without at least radioing in."

What also puzzles me about what happened to Team Garm are the actions, or inactions, of the interpreter. An experienced interpreter from the area, he would have known the men in the red Nissan car and he would have likely been able to gauge their purpose. So why did he stop?

I worry over this as our driver returns to the car. He speaks quickly with Tomasz and then starts up and we are again balancing along the unbearably narrow road.

I settle in for the ride back into Dushanbe and try not to think of the precarious shelf we are on. The "Great Game" was played in these very mountains, with British spies criss-crossing the tracks of Russian spies, each looking for the way to the land of spice and trade, India. Islam had met the Christian and the atheist West in these mountains, and come to understand the ruthlessness and military might that could be brought to bear for the sake of routes to gold, territory, and control. The names of Colonel Charles Stoddart and Captain Arthur Connolly are well remembered by Western historians. They were British officers who set out into Central Asia to form allegiances between Her Majesty and the local chieftains, open trade and find the routes to India through impossible heights. But they are not remembered by anyone in these mountains. They mark the meeting of disparate cultures and the mistrust of outsiders. Both Stoddart and Connolly were held in the emir of Buchara's dungeons for long months, subjected to torture, and finally beheaded. The British, with the most powerful army in the world at that time, could do nothing and did not even respond.

The lesson learned from these events is that outsiders cannot be eradicated from the region, but they can be stopped on a road they travel alone, away from their armies, and they can then be killed, one by one, or in fours.

VODKA

(Dushanbe, Tajikistan—November 1998)

In Tajikistan I learn to drink vodka. The Poles teach me. You drink by grasping the bottle (why waste a glass?) by the neck and swirl. Keep swirling until a funnel of rotating liquid develops. Keep swirling. When the vodka reaches its maximum speed, place the bottle quickly to your lips, invert, and a twisting tornado of alcohol will fire straight out, hit the back of your throat, career into your stomach, and then travel to your brain.

In Dushanbe vodka is sold in every store, on most street corners, and in every container you can imagine. It is sold in large and small glass bottles, one-litre plastic Coke bottles, yogurt containers, and tin cans. The cans are my favourite. They are black cans with a white skull and crossbones painted on. The brand is called Black Death, and even the most ardent drinkers fear it. It is cheap, a few pennies per eight-ounce can, affordable to the hard-up vodka drinkers, enticing them to give it a try.

While I am in the country, two Russian soldiers die from vodka poisoning. Vodka is consumed with fervour. Multiple bottles disappear at lunches and dinners. At celebrations, it is more seriously dispatched. Toast upon toast upon toast. Shot glasses clinking in the night. *Na zdorovia!*

Lenin has a park named after him in Dushanbe. His obsolete statue looks proudly off to a future that no longer exists. It is nestled comfortably in the large, very green park where on weekends the comrades came in past times to eat *lipioshka* with *shashlik*, drink vodka, and listen to the party speeches. They looked up to Lenin's firm but kindly face for inspiration and brought their children here. Small Ferris wheels whirled and bumper cars bumped and self-propelled metal mini-cars scraped across finish lines. Then the war came. The fighting in Dushanbe was street-to-street. Homes burned. Bodies lay in the gutters. People starved. Then the war paused, and has stayed paused to this day. The park is again alive with people eating *lipioshka* and *shashlik* and drinking vodka. Children laugh as they sit in the bumper cars. The Ferris wheel works intermittently and the Communist Party comrades are gone. Lenin is now alone.

I sit in this park in late November eating *shashlik*. Small metal tables are arranged under the trees, and it is pleasant sitting in the shade listening to the music from the overhead speakers, watching children running, and people, mostly men, apparently enjoying a leisurely afternoon. The children run in small groups from table to table. As they approach mine I see that some are without shoes and are in tattered clothes. These are the street children of Dushanbe. Their plight is desperate. They live in abandoned buildings and beg or steal for food or money, or work for older, teenage children selling chocolate bars or Kleenex packages, washing cars or carrying bags. They linger at street corners and knock on car windows, begging for money. They sell sunflower seeds, by the seed. Some live in an orphanage that is missing windows so that in winter when it snows outside, it also snows inside. One street boy who had a street mother was sold to a richer family who then exchanged him for their own son who had been arrested and placed in prison. The rich boy was set free. The poor boy imprisoned. Prison authorities needed someone in prison, it did not matter who. The poor boy was jailed for years, I was told.

There are street children and then there are street/war children. I have seen both. The former group lives a life of violence and fear, lacking consistent shelter, food, and protection, and the watch of gentle guardians. These children are on the fringes of mainstream society. The children raised on war also know the violence, the fear, the absence of shelter and guardians, but they know more. The children of war who live on the street exist outside a society in which order has itself collapsed and law is meaningless. They have seen and lived that society's devolution into violent despair and, without knowing why or how, they reflect the worst of what they see. It takes time for this to develop, for a war psychosis to take root.

I am not sure whether the Dushanbe children have developed such war psychosis. I have not seen it yet, but it may be there. I saw it in Phnom Penh. I watched a group of street children stone a cat to death. I watched a different group chase an insane woman who had stripped off her clothes and was running down the street screaming. The children were trying to hit her with rocks. And I have seen child soldiers, the Khmer Rouge children, looking grim-faced and clutching AK-47s.

The street children in Phnom Penh, not the child soldiers, were rounded up occasionally and placed in orphanages. Orphanages were walled mud compounds with one long bunkhouse for the children to sleep in. In the one I visited, children from six to sixteen were housed. Some had serious medical and psychiatric problems. One boy could not walk, so he crawled through the mud, dragging his limp limbs behind him. Another was dangerous to others and himself, we were told, and so had a heavy metal bar attached by a chain to one of his legs. It kept him from running away or throwing himself at another child.

At least one Western adoption agency that came to Cambodia never sought out children from such places. It only bought healthy babies from desperate families.

The medieval image of the chained boy remains with me as I watch these Tajik urchins scurry about. They approach me finally and I buy a chocolate bar. There is no stampede. They thank me and are off to the next table. Perhaps the war was not prolonged enough in Dushanbe to destroy the souls of these boys. I have not seen enough yet to know.

Vodka. At each table the men are drinking it, as are a few of the women. One man, a Russian-looking, ruddy-faced soldier in uniform, is extremely drunk. Staggering through the park, leaning on trees, he tries to catch his spinning world. He moves to the tables, a pilgrim travelling on his spirit quest from one table to another, always unwelcome. He is too drunk to reason with or shoo away. His hosts merely leave him at their table and go elsewhere. Alone, he lurches to the next. He is bad for business and *shashlik* sellers try unsuccessfully to discourage him.

Finally he stops at a table near mine. Two soldiers sit drinking vodka. They are sober and wear a uniform different from his. They don't look Russian. The CIS peacekeeping force in the country includes a number of Tajikistan's cousins. They may be from Kazakhstan or Uzbekistan, these two men. There is no love between the Russians and their partner armies. These two appear to have no patience for the drunk but will not leave their table. Faces reddening, they seem to be scolding him. The drunk is unarmed. The other two are carrying rifles.

As the three soldiers converse in vodka talk, a woman slides into an empty chair at a nearby table. She is tall, has big, man-like features, and is overloaded with makeup. She is intent on watching and listening to the soldiers. Her proximity and size make her an obvious intruder but the soldiers seem oblivious. Their exchange is heating up. One pushes his chair quickly away from the table and stands. He moves on the drunken Russian, forcing him to stand. Then, with a gentleness that surprises me, he leads the man towards the exit from the park. The drunk allows himself to be led. It is a friend taking a friend home. The woman is following them, not too discreetly. She too has a slight vodka wobble to her gait.

Outside the park the sober soldier deposits the drunk, now standing in the middle of a pedestrian walkway, abandoned and swaying. The woman leaves the park, passing the returning soldier, and heads directly for the Russian. He reminds me of an infant, unsteady head and shoulders, innocent in expectation. He waits for guidance. The slightest hint of direction and he will follow it. He has crawled into a vodka bottle a man and crawled out a baby, barely able to stand, legs wobbly, uncertain, unafraid, ready to be instructed. Who will direct him? Will it be good or evil? Time and circumstance will choose. At this time, during this moment, outside Lenin Park, on a warm fall day with music playing and children squealing and *shashlik* sizzling, unluckily for him it is evil that is present.

The woman moves to the soldier and grabs his arm, twirling him around towards the road. A car is waiting, black and box-like. She opens the rear door and guides him in. He does not resist. I strain to see if it is marked as a taxi. Pushing him into a taxi would be expected. Perhaps she is a prostitute and has seen easy work in him, a freshly paid soldier. I hope that is all it is.

The car has no taxi decals or roof mounting suggesting it is anything but a private car. In this city, that may mean nothing, however. Every car is a taxi for hire. But then she does something that tells me more. As she secures her catch in the back seat she stoops to follow him, but pauses for a heartbeat of time. Brief as it is, it is a powerful, clear indicator to me of intention. Prostitutes prowl this park and leave with men. No one cares. This woman, however, steals a glance to ensure she is not seen. Outside on the sidewalk, she has acted so fast in corralling her drunken Russian that pedestrians do not even turn in curiosity. But she needs to be sure. Content, she closes the door behind her and the car pulls away from the curb and joins the traffic. The soldier is gone, heading down Rudaki in a black box car, a woman with a man's features hovering over him, and vodka churning inside.

I stand and watch until the car disappears. Everything has happened so quickly that there is nothing I can do but stand and watch. Will he end up dead with his money gone, or just left in some ditch by the road, another victim of the criminal gangs that hunt easy targets in the parks of Dushanbe? I hope they show him mercy, is all I can think.

Vodka. From the Russian word for water, *voda*. Vodka is colourless, unaged liquor. It can stop your heart.

I met Ted in the early weeks of my arrival into Dushanbe in the bar built by the United Nations on top of the headquarters building. He was an American. He had survived Afghanistan, for many years working for humanitarian aid agencies. Afghanistan was the dark corner of the world. The Taliban were to be feared. The civil war that raged there touched everyone. Aid workers scrounged for their lives. Ted survived that.

I asked him about returning to the US and he told me he couldn't. He had been out too long, seen too much. The world back home was simply not enchanting enough, he said. But he was tired nonetheless. Tired of the bad food, and the absence of diversion (other than alcohol), and the strangeness, always the strangeness. He reckoned that the strangeness was in him now, and that he glowed with it. America was no longer a possibility. Like a fair number of the international aid workers I have met over time, he was forever trapped outside his home. In fact, he no longer had a home.

New Year's Eve, 1998. Kalashnikovs tracer bullets fired into the air. Where they fell nobody cared. Ted was at the UN party. He was drunk and I told the barmen to stop serving him. One hour later his mistress, vodka, led him out of the bar and to a steep stairway in the building. His mistress coursed through his veins. She didn't care that he had survived the civil war in Afghanistan and had made it through postwar Tajikistan or that, in service to the principles of peace and international order, he had abandoned his country and was homeless. Vodka couldn't care less. She took him to the head of the stairs and pushed him down so that he fell and crashed head-first into a pillar at the foot of the stairs and split open his skull and died. Vodka didn't care. She wanted another drink but couldn't have it so she left in anger and pushed Ted down the stairs.

BUZKASHI

(Dushanbe, Tajikistan—November 1998)

In the morning, the raucous cawing of a mass of birds heading out of the city flying over my building triggers an explosion inside my head. The explosion is the beer-and-vodka depth charge going off and blowing away my frontal lobe. An acid has been released in that explosion and begins to sear through the other lobe, chewing and burning its way into my left eye. Pressing a pillow to my temple I try squeezing out the acid that is poisoning me. I wish to regain unconsciousness. The birds caw on, screaming at each other and at me, keeping me awake and in profound pain. I am going to die, I think. You *are* dead, the crows sing. They are already pecking at my eyeballs.

It is a hangover of epic proportions. A perfect hangover. I will remember this hangover for the rest of my life, I decide, and never, and I mean never, take another drink. I begin to think I may have actually been poisoned. Russian soldiers have died from drinking bad vodka. I am dying too.

At last the crows move on.

I am suffering from a night out with my Polish colleagues. I learned the previous night, under the close tutelage of the Polish military, how to drink a vodka depth charge. A small glass of vodka is plunged into a jar of beer, at which point the victim downs the mixture in several furious gulps. Jozef and Wiktor applauded my first.

"Ronald, good," said Wiktor. "Now come with us to a party."

With my help, they had finished a bottle of vodka at the Embassy bar, then had gone to a restaurant and ordered a fresh bottle. Bottle finished, they stood and announced, "Now for the party ..."

"What party?" I asked.

"Come with us. You must finally see Dushanbe."

We ended up at a side door of a building on a street that was outside our safety zone and my comfort zone.

"I think I should go home," I said.

"Nonsense! Come in. Have fun." Wiktor, now very drunk, wrapped his tree-trunk arm around my neck and pulled me in through the door. The shadowy figures of two women stepped aside to let us through. Inside, two tables sat in a small and otherwise barren, ugly room that smelled vaguely of disinfectant and feet. A curtain hung over a doorway into a second room.

"Vodka!" Jozef called out. The shadow women walked through the curtain and came back with a bottle and some glasses. As the curtain moved I saw a bare mattress without blankets or sheets on the floor in the next room.

Neither woman was particularly attractive. They both had large heads and long, wide faces. They were big women and the thought crossed my mind for a moment that they might be men.

As with most Tajiks, their facial skin bore the signs of bad water and frequent washing with harsh soap. A thick, hide-like quality had developed. They had facial hairs and bushy eyebrows and were dressed in gypsy clothes, long skirts and blouses with puffy sleeves that covered their arms to the wrists. Their feet were bare. Neither seemed particularly happy to see us but they were accommodating, retrieving the vodka at Jozef's command and rising to dance when Wiktor said, "Let's dance."

I stood watching the four of them in a slow teetering dance with no music, rocking back and forth, clutching and circling like dancing bears. The women's ankles, the size of melons, exposed with the slow twirls. I finally announced that I would leave. "Goodbye, Ronald," one of the bears called over the shoulder of his partner.

I left my very drunk Polish friends, the smell of Lysol and feet and the spectacle of the dancing bears.

Pulling myself out of bed, I shuffle to the kitchen and drink long and deeply from a bottle of ice-cold water in my fridge. My head pounds and I feel sick. I shuffle back to bed.

I try to sleep, but I can't. The pounding in my head intensifies. My heartbeat pulsates through my veins, into my head. Boom. Boom. Boom. No, not that, it is outside me and in my room, a hammering on a wall. The neighbour's wall. Construction on Saturday morning! Shit. I pile the pillows on my head and curse them to hell. I am sick. Stop it. But now the banging sounds hollow, and vaguely metallic. My front door. Someone is banging on my front door. Sitting up in bed I feel the room spin. Jesus Christ, go away. Boom. Boom. Boom. Now faint voices join in, between the booms. I stagger to the door and pull back the bolt. Clang. On the other side, two men, clean-shaven, smiling.

"Oh, God ... what do you want?" I shuffle back down the hall, leaving the door open for them.

Tomasz laughs, but his face is serious. "Ronald, you look bad, my friend. Oh...."

"You look like shit," adds Felix, a UN civilian police officer. "And you stink." He pulls his tunic up over his nose. "Take a bath."

"What happened to you? Is she still here?"

"No woman." I am in the kitchen with the water bottle. "You Poles did this to me."

"Vodka," he says shaking his head. "Poison." Tomasz never drinks, and he regards those who do with mild amusement and warm disdain. "Have coffee. A shower. Then come with us. We have good news for you. You will thank us for this. One day." He laughs at my discomfort.

I finish the water and the two men follow me to a couch in the front room. I lie on it.

"Very good news," says Felix, tunic still up over his nose.

They stand over me. Tomasz is grinning.

"The mission is cancelled and we can go home," I say.

"That would be a disaster," says Tomasz. "Be serious."

They both wait, expecting me to try a few guesses.

"I'm too sick for this game. Tell me."

"We have found it," Tomasz finally says. "We have found your game."

Head swollen and slow with the cotton of a hangover I say, "My game. Is what?"

"*Buzkashi*, Ronald. *Buzkashi*. We have found a game. Today, a wedding celebration. We will go. Shower, get dressed, we go now. It is outside city. Not far, but outside. We must leave and return while it is still light."

The vodka has absorbed all my water and my lips are dry again. Someone has stolen a piece of my clothing, wrapped it a round a voodoo doll and at this moment is sticking a pin in its eye. But holding my head, pushing my palm into my eye to stem the pain, I shuffle back to the kitchen for another drink of water, and then the sickness comes and I rush back to the bathroom and kneel before the toilet. My legs shake as I struggle to stand and I imagine a ride in a Land Cruiser over torturous roads to get to a *Buzkashi* game and immediately bend back to the bowl for another round.

But how can I miss this chance? Omar Sharif riding with a broken leg and scooping up a headless goat amidst a crush of fierce men and lathering horses. "Give me a minute," I shout to them.

"You stink," Felix shouts back.

Buzkashi!

As we bump our way along the narrow, slanted path to the field, we can just begin to make out the thunder of hooves over the hard, dry ground. We crest the top of the path and get our first glimpse of the game. Clouds of dust rise like smoke around a large scrum of horses. The scrum is a densely packed press of the animals. At the outer edges, some riders sit rigidly upright, apparently content to wait out the battle that is then taking place among others at the epicentre where heads and torsos bob and weave. After parking our vehicle, we silently take our places on the side of a hill where most spectators either sit on the ground or stand. The game is hypnotic to watch. It is so thoroughly strange and unexpected a sight that we find ourselves unwilling at first to break the enchantment with words.

So we sit in silence, and watch an ancient tradition play out on the field below.

The pack begins to twirl as the horses on the periphery move sideways, spinning the others. With the motion, gaps between mounts appear and riders immediately lean off their saddles, bending as far to the ground as possible without falling off. Then, like a top whose string has been slowly pulled, the scrum spins open and the rings of horses peel away until one horse and rider emerge. And he is riding hard. Whip held firmly between his teeth, the rider has found a clear way through the scrum and with one hand halfway to the ground, grasps a large mass of black fur and drags and bumps it along. He has the goat, and with the other hand on the reins of the horse and his feet digging into its hindquarters, he is charging out of the tangle and into the open field. The others give chase and the game is on. His objective is a line of rope lying on the ground halfway up the hill we sit upon, and only a metre or two in front of us. But the rider doesn't head our way. He first gathers speed over the open valley, taking him further away from the finish line, then circles around, with several horses close on his heels, and begins a long, hard, ferocious gallop straight at us. He doesn't make it to us. Small clusters of horses and riders have formed near the finish line and others are angled into him, forcing him away from the line and into one of the clusters, until he slows and then stops and a tugging for the goat begins. Dozens of horses and riders are in this game, and as we watch we can see alliances constantly form and disband in an instant, up to the very goal line. Horses and riders criss-crossing, cutting off, ramming. Small whips are used on the horses and, close in, on opponents. Most of the riders wear the soft shell-like helmets used by Russian tank drivers to keep from gashing their heads inside the sharp-edged surfaces of their tanks. A referee rides along with the group, occasionally blowing a whistle, but the rules are not apparent. When victory comes out of the clouds and up the hill to the finish line, no one cheers except the winner. Money has been wagered hard and lost. And then the game starts again.

Nothing I have seen in my cloistered life in central Dushanbe, or read about from the bunker that was UN headquarters, felt or looked like this. It is Central Asia in front of me, galloping by, and it makes me shiver. The horses pound over the ground. Their riders, whips and, sometimes, reins between their teeth, reach for a hold on the goat.

"It makes meat easy for eating," a young Tajik man sitting on the hill beside us finally says, breaking our silence and awe by trying to explain the game with the few words in English he knows.

He explains: "A wedding reception follow game and the goat that has been pulled and dropped and walked on by horses is used for feast. The game makes it easier to eat."

"I don't believe it," I say to our impromptu friend.

Before he can respond, the horses are charging towards us again. A rider reaches our hill and is climbing. The field of play is about half a kilometre long, and bowl-shaped, with a river through it and a discarded school bus parked in the middle, children crawling over it. The horses stay away from the bus.

I ask our new friend, "How do they win?"

"Winner is declared when someone carries goat over the line." He motions a few metres in front of us.

The mass of horses turns and is now bearing down on the finish line. Tomasz says, "Time to go," and turns and runs up the hill. I wait for the locals to move and when they do I turn and run with them up the hill. A pack of forty or fifty horses and riders is climbing the hill in very hot pursuit of the leader, now straining to keep hold of the goat. His own confederates are trying to slow the attackers, so their man can win and share the prize with them. We are close enough to sense breath and slobber, and to see the horses straining hard to climb up, haunches low and front legs extended to gain the slope. The people are screaming as they run from the line. Some are laughing.

The origins of *Buzkashi* are sketchy, but it appears to have arisen first on the plains of Mongolia as a means of keeping warriors sharp between battles. It was also said to have first used prisoners of war in place of the goats, dismembering and pulverizing them through the course of play. The violence of the game is readily apparent: the use of whips, the collisions, and the tug-of-wars that ensue over who carries the goat. Riders fall from their horses and usually the hooves move with great care to avoid the downed man. The skill of riders and horses is remarkable. But it is a fast, brutal game, filled with close calls, injuries, and in the game I witnessed, death. We watch, helpless, as a rider is knocked from his horse at full gallop and rolls and bounces onto the ground. He lies still for a moment and then as he slowly stands we cheer. But the horse has been in full gallop when his rider falls and the animal continues to run hard without him. Some of the spectators are on the field itself and scatter from the charge of animals when they have to. A boy, ten or twelve at most, is on the field, his back to the lone horse running hell-bent away from the game. I watch the two and stand. "Oh my god," I say, "it's heading right for him." Others on the hill next to me see it too and they stand and point, but that is all the time we have. The horse rams the boy at full gallop and throws him up and forward and then runs over him. I see the tangle of his arms and legs under the horse and then when he emerges and the horse has passed over him, his body is flat out on the ground, motionless. A man runs to him and lifts him. The boy's arms and legs hang limply down and I fear the worst has happened.

The game pauses, the riders hold their mounts tight for less than a minute as the boy is carried off, and then the game is on again and someone has the dead goat and is breaking for the finish line.

But for us, the game truly is over. Around me the crowd has gone silent, but no one moves from where they sit. "He is dead," says our newfound interpreter. "I am sure of it." We all three nod to him. Death is too commonplace in Tajikistan and not frightening enough to stop a *Buzkashi* game from continuing, or its fans from leaving.

Tomasz says, "We have to go."

"I agree," I say.

Understanding that I could not have known why he had suggested it, Tomasz says, "No. Not for that. In this crowd I see Kalashnikovs. These are fighters," he continues, using the term we use for any one of the armed opposition groups. "They have seen us and are talking among each other. We must leave now."

There is no debate or questioning of what he says. Felix and I stand immediately and follow Tomasz off the hill and towards our Land Cruiser. Regardless of the political stability of the moment, the possibility of being kidnapped for ransom always exists. Along with *Buzkashi*, it remains a Central Asian tradition and we are prime targets.

We leave the game hurriedly, shaken by the image of the boy, and when we are off the hill and near our vehicle my body remembers the vodka: I bend over and throw up.

"Nice," Felix says walking past me. "Lawyer. Ha!"

The pain in my stomach and the uncontrollable urgings to vomit feel a strange relief against what has just happened out on the field. The accident is one part; the reaction of those gathered to it quite another. A moment's hesitation and the game resumed. Just another dead boy in a land of dead boys. It was a harsh life that produced the game of *Buzkashi*, and a harder one still that produced the muted emotions to the death of a boy.

What I do not know at that uncomfortable moment as I struggle to regain my composure, is that the *Buzkashi* game we have just witnessed will be my last glimpse of authentic Tajik culture, untrammelled, uncorrupted, and uncensored. As I come to learn, the rest will be a performance.

III.
KILLINGS IN CAMBODIA 1992–1993

THERE IS A GHOST IN YOUR ROOM
(Phnom Penh, Cambodia—1992)

"The UN will never understand this country, because they do not believe in ghosts." So disclosed an Italian journalist writing for *Der Spiegel* one morning in 1992 in the lobby of the Hotel Le Royale, where journalists and UNists like me gathered each morning in Phnom Penh.

The journalist's pronouncement was made on a hot morning some weeks after a troupe of United Nations players and I had arrived in our new country of residence. It was prompted by a dream I had had the night before and my very vocal preoccupation with that dream. It had frightened me.

The nightmare featured one harrowing scene. I was standing in a room like my own, Room 314. Beside me was a boy I knew to be my son, although I had no child. He had blond hair and blue eyes and I held his hand. In the middle of the room, standing like a great misty castle, was a large four-poster bed. Over the bed hung a white gauze mosquito netting that billowed and contracted the surface of the netting so that it appeared that a great monster on the bed was breathing in and out. Suddenly, a woman emerged from behind the gauze and began walking around the castle until she came to a chair. The chair was propped against the wall adjacent to the one the boy and I stood against. We then had a clear look at the woman. Climbing onto the chair the woman cast a fleeting look our way and then she smiled. I knew her in this dream life to be my wife. Reaching above, she produced the looped end of a rope and pulled it over her head and around her neck. She then stepped off the chair and swung from her neck. I gasped with horror at what was happening yet could do nothing. The boy began to cry. He continued crying as he watched his mother die, swinging in small circles in front of him. Mercifully, I then awoke.

I lay awake for hours afterward, drenched in sweat, yet cold with the chill on my nerves. Although I did manage to fall asleep again, the dream returned several times that night, until I was edgy with fear of it and reluctant to close my eyes. The next morning in the lobby I told the story to a number of those gathered, including the Italian. He had lived and worked in Cambodia for years.

"There is a ghost in your room," he said to me afterwards.

"It was a dream," I said, "not a visitation."

"My young friend," he said, "the dreams you have here, in this place where so much blood has spilled, will not be restful. Believe in ghosts, Ronald, or they will haunt you."

I laughed at his serious expression and dismissed his comments as those of an expat gone native to the mysticism of Asia.

The next night I had the dream again. The images were so clear that to this day I can see and remember them in detail. The woman's night dress fluttering as she died. The boy's eyes glistening with tears. I had believed throughout my life that a living God had been nailed to wood beams and had come back to life after three days entombed. Why were ghosts in Cambodia any less real?

I left the ghosts of room 314 and went on an assignment out of Phnom Penh. A local dispute over land had turned into a demonstration and a shooting in the village of Phoum Deum Svey. A man had died and the UN sent investigators to find out why, as allegations had been made that the police had fired into a peaceful crowd. A fundamental component of a society in which basic rights were respected is one in which people can meet and demonstrate without the fear of being shot at. Shooting a demonstrator is a violation of a basic human right, so within the UN jurisdiction and mandate.

I led the investigation team, made up of myself and another human rights officer, a very eager American boy, Jamie, who spoke some Khmer, smoked a pipe in university, and was on his way to Harvard law school. With us were two French gendarmes and an interpreter. It was my first foray into rural Cambodia, and the United Nations' first police and human rights action in the country.

Cambodia in 1992 was still a highly controlled country under a Stalinist style of governance. Movement from one district to the next was strictly monitored and undertaken only with permission. It was at the district level that local power lay. Police and military were under the district committees. They tended to be hard-line party ideologues, often former combat veterans.

Protocol required that we report at the district office on arrival into the area. We didn't, because initial reports of the killings suggested police and local official involvement. Our inquiries would have been compromised, we believed, if we went through local government channels.

The beauty of Cambodia is not in its temples carved from the jungle at Angkor, or the glitter of the Royal Palace in Phnom Penh, or the great Tonle Sap Lake, whose flow of water changes direction each year. Beauty in Cambodia lies within the peasants' titanic daily struggle for survival. They break their backs in the rice paddies, bending and pulling and squatting from first light to last. Push the water buffalo into the mud and push him harder to plow a new line for planting rice. In bad soil, in droughts that dry up hope, in monsoons that wash away everything, in the shadows of tanks, the peasants forge the heart and soul of the country.

When the peasantry of this Cambodian village saw us arrive, many could only stare in disbelief at us. Most had heard that the United Nations was in their country, but they had not seen us yet, not here, in the rice fields and in the heartlands. Isolated from the outside, they rarely saw outsiders, rarer still white men walking among them. There we were, pasty and dripping with heat. The American, the two French gendarmes, and me. Chino trousers, double-pocketed British explorer-man shirts, and French gendarmes' uniforms were no use against the fireball that was consuming our fatty tissue by the second.

A big, noisy Land Cruiser sprayed rocks and mud and vanity. We disembarked and walked between the rows of huts to demonstrate our affinity for the villagers and respect for their way of life. Crowds followed us, first to the headman's hut, where we introduced ourselves, then on to each of those we visited.

Men in the village were bare-chested and wore coloured skirts. The women wore identical-looking skirts, but also wore a length of the same fabric to conceal their breasts. Naked children criss-crossed our paths or swarmed together like bees. Every now and then, one would swoop in for a touch and a giggle. They pointed at us and bounced up and down. Some of the children had oozing sores in their eyes and seemed to be partially blind.

The village was made up of perpendicular dirt roads. On each road stood a line of thatch and bamboo huts, each one raised some ten metres above ground to allow a breeze to find its way up and through the bamboo-lashed flooring and into the chambers above. Hammocks swung lazily underneath. Running in a Marx Brothers' pandemonium, chickens scattered one way, then the next. And standing silent and indomitably still, water buffaloes watched us pass with their big, beautiful eyes.

Our plan was to move from hut to hut looking for witnesses to the shooting, starting with the families of the dead.

I had believed we were embarking on a futile enterprise. Dropping as we did from the outside, we would return to the outside and leave those who spoke to us alone and vulnerable. Every conversation would be watched. Every name remembered. Isolated from the reaches of Phnom Penh, the villagers had to survive by their own guile and resiliency, just as they had throughout long years of Maoist Pol Pot scrutiny, then Vietnamese Stalinism. How could we expect them to reveal the truth of what had happened, particularly if that truth pointed to the government?

Cambodian villages do not have street signs and house numbers. Everyone knows where everyone else lives. To find the families of the shooting victims we had to stop and ask, and stop and ask, and stop and ask. The markers of geography by which the residents knew how to find someone's hut did not resonate in our occidental brains, or in that of Sangna, our Phnom Penh interpreter. "They live around that corner," said a girl we stopped to ask. After turning the corner and walking for ten minutes we stopped again. "Very close to here," one person said, "Go to big hut by palm tree and then turn this way. But why not drive?" Another said, "Other side of village, sir. Not near here." Most people we asked laughed when we spoke to them. They seemed to be delighting in the act of talking to big, white, sweaty strangers wearing the wrong clothes.

Finally, we decided to take a hostage, a girl of perhaps twelve. "Ask her if she would come with us," I said to Sangna. "Ask her if she can show us where." Giggling with delight she led the way.

When we arrived at the hut of the victim's family, we found a silent group of worried faces. This is because the Khmer mourn in silence. Their tears are shed in solitude and are not for public sympathies. Sangna gingerly approached. "They will not speak, sir," he said, returning. "It is too much for them now."

"I understand," I said. "This may be futile." I turned to walk away when Sangna stopped me.

"Sir," he said. "They say you look hot and why not have a coconut? It is a good idea, Mr. Ron. Very good." I pried my parched lips apart to accept the invitation, thinking only of liquid to stay a relentless thirst. I was too exhausted from the heat at first to understand the subtle gesture.

Sitting heavily on a stump outside the hut, I watched a machete swung deftly again and again until a lid popped off a king coconut. Liquid brimmed to the surface of the opening and ran down the side. My mouth ached. Handing me the lime green bowling-ball-sized orb the village man smiled at me and nodded. I sipped and then I drank, long and hard, at the sweet nectar of the king. The king coconut contains at least a litre or more of juice. I drank it all, savouring the sweet coconut taste and the vast amount of warm yet cooling liquid. At last I put it down, looked up, and saw the smiling faces of the family looking at me. Some laughed and pointed. Others clapped. "Thank you," I said. "I am saved."

As a second coconut was sliced for me and for the others in my group, the uncle of the family sat with us. "Land is important to us," he began. "We toil and work hard. It is everything. They are trying to take our land." He paused and looked down at a line in the dry dirt he had been etching with a stick. We sat silently as he drew with the stick. At first I thought he was drawing a map or diagram of what had happened. I then realized it was just a long, slow doodle as he appeared to be weighing the merits of trusting us. It turned out he waited too long.

Cambodian police, in their pristine dry coconut-green shirts and red striped pants, suddenly appeared around us. I immediately thought of bell-boys and waiters at a beach hotel, dressed to resemble green swizzle sticks to match the chunky fruit rum drinks they delivered to thirsty tourists. One approached, smiled at me and asked in Khmer, "Another drink, sir?"

Sangna translated. "He asks, 'What are you doing here?'"

The captain, immediately in front of me, was a head shorter than I, and though he smiled, it was a thin tight curl that came across his face more a challenge than a greeting.

"We are members of the UN," I said. "We are here about the shooting."

As I waited for the translation, I saw that my French gendarmes had taken up what appeared to be positions opposite the twelve or more well-armed police arrayed against us. Unarmed, the French Gendarmes appeared to be trying to stand as tall as they could, staring hard and with righteous purpose at the police. Jesus, I thought. Are they that stupid?

Sangna looked at me and smiled. "Mr. Ron, he says something like, 'That is nice. Now go away.'"

"Please tell him that I can't. I have my instructions to carry out an investigation into the killings here and produce a report. Under the UN mandate, we have jurisdiction to monitor human rights abuses in the country and to take corrective action if we see it necessary. I am here, with my colleagues, to determine what happened two nights ago and to decide if the matter requires UN attention. Please tell him this, Sangna." I folded my arms triumphantly with the solid conviction of the angel Gabriel.

"I cannot," said Sangna after a pause.

"Why not? It is correct and it is the law under the Peace Accord," I responded, ready to do battle.

"Yes," said Sangna. "Maybe. But I not understand one word. Please, repeat. Very slow. Peace what?"

For close to an hour, through translation that may or may not have expressed what I had to say, I argued with the police captain. At this stage of the UN intervention in Cambodia, only a small contingent had yet arrived, and though jurisdiction to investigate and travel freely was entrenched in the Peace Accord, the practice had yet to start. We were the first, and for this Cambodian police unit, the first was too many.

"You must go," the captain kept saying. "You need permission to be here. If you have permission, I welcome you."

"And if we don't leave?" I asked.

His smile broadened and he turned and walked back to the group of his fellow officers. They seemed so young and grim, with their sharp glances at us and at the villagers. There was evident bad blood between the two groups, caused, I assumed, by the shooting. A radio crackled and the captain bent his head in conversation.

When I had driven into the village with my powder-blue French escorts and the American Ivy Leaguer, I knew almost nothing of Khmer culture, little of its grassroots politics, and less than I thought of my true capacity to sweat. I learned about each that afternoon. With orders to investigate a murder and clutching a copy of the Peace Accord, I was now the lead United Nations human rights investigator in the field in Cambodia. But what should I do now?

Ask a Cambodian, a voice inside me said. He might know what to do in Cambodia. I turned to Sangna. "Should we leave, Sangna? Or push this?"

"Leave," he said without hesitation.

"Why?" I asked.

"They will arrest us," came his reply. "Or they will shoot us."

"Do you think they would?"

He looked at me and laughed, "Why not? We are here. In front of people they must control." He spread his hands out to the village. "We must be obedient to them. Or they lose face. If I were them, I would arrest us."

The captain was returning, two rifle-toting men at his side. He was not smiling.

"And so?" he asked Sangna.

Sangna translated and then looked to me. I fumbled out, "Tell him we will return tomorrow and ... that nothing should happen to those we spoke to in this village." I was uneasy now, feeling weak and vulnerable. We were giving in, in the first test of our authority. What solace could the villagers take in this?

Sangna said, "He says good. See you tomorrow." The captain then backed up with his troop of men, enough to allow us passage out of the village.

I wondered if we were making a grave mistake in leaving these people.

So I said, "Sangna, discreetly take the names of those we spoke with. I want them to be here when we return tomorrow."

"Yes, sure," he said, and skipped off.

A senior UN political officer once said to me that out in the field, far from the power of the Security Council or NATO jets or governments, the work of the UN is about persuasion, bluff, charm, and luck. Out there, on the limb, you can't make it work by imposing embargoes or dropping bombs. You have to convince the person opposite that your way is better and then you have to hope to God it is. You use reason, emotion, history, tears, and everything else you can think of. Never go too far, never make someone want to shoot you, or anyone else, he said. Getting shot never helps peace.

We drove back down the route to Phnom Penh as the evening amber danced over and through the dust kicked up off the road. What a beautiful sight, I thought as I watched emerald-green rice stalks catching the orangey lickings of sunlight descending. A water buffalo stood up to its knees in water in one rice paddy, languidly chewing straw and grass it had ripped out of the water. "Keep going," it seemed to be saying as it watched me with fluttering eyelids and long slow chews. "Keep going before it's too late."

PALE BLUE HOPE
(Phnom Penh, Cambodia—April 1992)

The early days of the United Nations Transitional Authority for Cambodia in Cambodia, when the new UN flags were being unfurled and the light blue hats were bobbing up and down for the first time on the city streets, gave everyone hope that peace had finally come. It was pale blue hope.

I stood with my interpreter Sangna by the side of the road with the people of Phnom Penh watching the first peacekeeping military contingents arriving. Armoured personnel carriers freshly painted white. Pale blue or black lettering: *United Nations*. Flags fluttering and steely-eyed young soldiers in camouflage fatigues. People in the street stopped to gape. A group of teenage girls next to me huddled together giggling and pointing—at me, at the Australian soldiers. Cyclo drivers froze in mid-pedal. The West had come to them, finally, and just as they had imagined. In shiny new vehicles, painted white. Young fresh faces. Hope and honesty and Christianity—rolling down their streets. Finally, peace.

"What do you think? How does this make you feel?" I asked Sangna then, when the United Nations blue was still a fresh presence in the country.

He smiled at me and nodded. "Happy," he said. "Happy and safe. It is over. This tells me that, at last, war is over."

"Right. Over. For how long?" I asked.

He puffed on a cigarette that seemed perpetually lit and said, "The people believe. The Western governments are rich and strong. They can make real peace here." Discarding the remainders of his cigarette with a vigorous flick of his fingers, he added, "I hope ... this is our last chance. It cannot fail. If it does, the Khmer Rouge will rise again. That is for certain true."

I nodded and said, "For this to work, really work, these soldiers may have to stay forever."

He blushed and smiled. "Of course," he said. "That is also my hope."

In Cambodia in 1992 the political leaders needed a persistent yet relatively harmless war to maintain a hold on armies and generals and money. But the people, those like my Cambodian friend, wanted the conflict to end and they saw only one solution. That solution came from outside. For him, and others I came to know in the country, they could not care less that foreign troops would be on their soil to maintain peace and that Cambodians could not manage it without them. National pride had been scraped away by long years of war, poverty, corruption, and deceit. A people's history of resistance to foreign influx was suddenly replaced by a plea: "Save us from ourselves!"

The day after we had been ousted from Phoum Deum Svey village, I was lingering in Phnom Penh waiting for political muscle to flex and for our negotiated return to the village, to the investigation of the killing of the peasant protesters.

What had happened to us in that Cambodian village had drawn considerable attention from the UN hierarchy, the Cambodian President Hun Sen, and the international press. Western diplomats scurried from meeting to meeting with the frenetic pace of cockroaches darting from fridge to stove and back. Twenty thousand UN personnel, thousands of trucks, Land Cruisers, motorcycles, boats, helicopters, cargo planes, jets, prefabricated houses, and a budget of over $1.5 billion, were standing by. The way out of a war in which the interests of the Khmer Rouge and the Western powers, including the US, were uncomfortably similar, looked to be in jeopardy. In Phnom

Penh, there was an atmosphere of shock and deep concern in the diplomatic corps and the United Nations leadership.

As for me, my lone thought as I meandered down the road that morning was the slaking succulence of that wonderful coconut. The feel of that refreshing juice lingered in my mouth and throat, which had been parched since I stepped off the plane into Cambodia. A thirst had been created that I thought would never diminish. Until then.

International politics was no match for reminiscence of a great thirst doused.

I wandered the streets of Phnom Penh with Sangna—precious time for me to learn more of the country.

We ended up in Tuol Sleng, the former school that had become an interrogation centre and death camp during Pol Pot's reign. "Hundreds of Pol Pot's suspected enemies were tortured and killed here," the inscription on the wall reads. It is a museum now. The cells are intact, left as they were on the day the Vietnamese liberators arrived. Dark red stains on the floors, steel beds on which prisoners were manacled and electrocuted. "Confess your disloyalty," they had each been told. One hundred volts and they did. Rows of pictures of frightened prisoners, boys and girls, line the walls. "They were tortured here," the inscription says; "they were killed here."

On one wall are the confessions. One is a handwritten confession tortured out of a Westerner whose bad luck led his sailboat into Cambodian waters and Khmer Rouge hands. He died after confessing to working as a spy for the CIA.

Human skulls decorate a giant map of Cambodia in the foyer.

"Two million dead," the banner reads.

Reminders of Pol Pot's brutality are everywhere. Taught in school, broadcast on radio, referred to daily in newsprint. When the United Nations arrived, the people of Cambodia had not been allowed the healing powers of distance and forgetting. The war that continued after Pol Pot's Khmer Rouge fell required a certain rigidity of resolve and purpose. A Vietnamese army had remained in Cambodia, tolerated by a populace who despised the Khmer Rouge more than they did the Vietnamese, but only barely. The Vietnamese occupiers and their Cambodian puppet government had to maintain the presence of Pol Pot's historical record in the mind of the people, lest they forget and begin wondering why their historical adversary, the Vietnamese, were still at every corner.

"We had no corruption, before," Sangna announced to me.

"Before what?" I asked him.

"Before the Vietnamese."

"Really."

"Yes," he said. "Also prostitution. We had none. The Vietnamese brought that. Prostitutes are Vietnamese, not Khmer."

"I don't think you're right," I said to him. "They are in my hotel and some are Khmer."

"No, sir," he said. "Cannot be."

"Yes," I said.

"No." He smiled, then thought for a moment before finally almost shouting, "They are corrupted. By the Vietnamese!"

The pressure of being forced to remember the horror of that war weighed on the psyche of Cambodians. They were compelled by the government's propaganda campaign to remain afraid, every day, for years after the fall of the Khmer Rouge and throughout the protracted civil war that followed. I later saw the impact this propaganda campaign had on a Cambodian girl working in the house a group of us had rented in Phnom Penh. Her name was Pinh and she was seventeen years old when we met her. She came each day to clean and do laundry for us. One day, while she was working in the house, a policeman arrived. He was her suitor, accepted by the family and eager to wed her. But Pinh didn't love him and had refused to marry him. She had been beaten by her sisters for refusing. The policeman was a man of means and influence and could not be easily rebuffed. When our household came to know what was happening, we intervened, innocently, naively, stupidly. At this stage, we were actively engaged in a daily battle against the Cambodian police and had come to see them as dull, corrupt, and brutal. We eagerly told her she could live with us, free from her family and this man. She quickly accepted and moved in.

Then one day, she disappeared. She had left our home on a weekend to visit friends and had not returned. It was not like her. We went to her family. They had not seen her. We went to the jilted policeman, ready for a confrontation. But upon hearing the news, he seemed genuinely disturbed and determined to help find her. We went to hospitals and police stations throughout the city, looking. At night, we drove back streets. Our worst fears preyed on our minds. I was convinced that a pretty Khmer girl would not just vanish without someone initiating the vanishing.

On the third day following her disappearance, I was sitting at the breakfast table when a neighbour came to our door.

"There is girl here," he said to me as I opened the door. He pointed to a bench at the corner of our veranda. Pinh sat, swinging her legs.

"Pinh!" I called. She did not respond. Her legs kept swinging.

I walked towards her. She stared straight ahead. "Pinh," I said softly. She began speaking in Khmer. "What is she saying?" I asked my neighbour.

"The same as she has said all morning, and for many days before," he replied, "She say that Pol Pot is coming and that we will all die."

"Many days before? Before she disappeared?"

"Yes. Yes. We hear her working in the day. She talk about Pol Pot. Every day. Now she cry," my neighbour said. Pinh's hair was matted with dirt and her dress dusty and patched with brown stains of mud.

"Now she calls you Prince Sihanouk," said the neighbor. "She says you will die. Pol Pot will kill you too. Crazy." He shook his head.

The words of Hun Sen's government, at that moment in power in Cambodia, came back to me then. "Never forget, boys and girls, when you close your eyes at night a monster lurks outside the window. Never forget." It had driven her crazy.

We drove her home that afternoon and left her with her father and mother. They cradled her and stroked her head. Her mother and sisters cried. Her father shook his head. They blamed us, I knew, for new and confusing ideas that had clouded their daughter's mind and driven her mad, in the end. As we drove away from their house I glanced back and saw her quickly wave at me. "Prince Sihanouk," she said as she waved. "Goodbye. Goodbye."

Goodbye, Pinh.

WHAT HAPPENED TO YOUR WATCH?
(Cambodia—April 1992)

Cambodia was heat and dark nights and the clack of rice sellers' batons and monkeys on my windowsill, flooded streets that rose over truck bonnets, and thick, slippery mud that made car wheels spin and slide. It was flies on undercooked pork and watery marijuana soup. It was a soufflé that I ordered as I first sat at the Intercontinental restaurant and that arrived light and delicious hours later. It was warm beer with ice cubes and a smile that cracked open and took over a brown moon-shaped face and children giggling and sliding, slippery, over and around their father in a pool of shallow water under a bridge. Cambodia was rice fields and water buffaloes and a rumour of a herd of a thousand elephants seen in the north. It was sweltering nights and gins and tonics and vodka with chilies and lying drenched with sweat every night and waking up drenched with sweat every morning and then eating a heaping bowl of chilies and onions and noodles that somehow kept me cool and iced coffee with condensed milk and giant papayas and endless shapes of bananas and rats as large as cats. It was meeting Hun Sen and arguing with him over the treatment of refugee returnees and it was meeting Prince Sihanouk and his Korean bodyguards and having him embrace and kiss me. Cambodia was lines of people waiting for hours on their first-ever election day and it was UN helicopters hovering protectively over polling stations.

These wonders were, for me, Cambodia. But something else lingered. The price of peace was heavy, for some, and those who embraced it too early, when the promise remained unfulfilled, had paid that price. I saw the secret prisons, and the marks of torture and the dead, and when I reminisce, I see those faces first.

And those faces began, for me, in Phoum Deum Svey village, east of Phnom Penh City.

Cambodian potholes are craters as large as roads. A journey across country in a Land Cruiser is like being on one end of a teeter-totter facing a demonic child with piston legs. A jarring motion up, a jarring motion down, a constant discomfort. The roads east of Phnom Penh had been bombed by the Americans and bombed by the Vietnamese and never repaired. Twisted bridges lay beside makeshift bridges that had to be jerry-built for any commerce to move down the road. The crater potholes remained.

As we bounced along, my thoughts turned to the villagers we had left behind, and how vulnerable we had left them in speaking so openly. I hoped no one had faced retribution for my blunder of openness. I would not make the same mistake again.

We returned to the village forty-eight hours after police had asked us to leave, when negotiators had reminded Hun Sen's government that an international agreement had been signed that allowed us free access to the entire country. For his part, in Phnom Penh, Hun Sen, in meetings he had with senior United Nations officials, accused me of breaching protocol and of not informing the local authorities of our arrival in Phoum Deum Svey village.

By the time we reached the district police station outside the village, the effect of clenching and unclenching my teeth and of my head repeatedly smashing into the side window of the Land Cruiser left me weary. It was 1 p.m. and forty-plus degrees Celsius and inside the frigid environment of the air-conditioned Land Cruiser, I was sweating buckets.

I was convinced that the police would be hostile and uncooperative, resentful of being told by authorities in Phnom Penh to allow us access to their domain. I was also sure that a display of power of some form would be arranged inside the mould-stained building to greet us. Police in dress uniforms. The district chief in his finest. That kind of thing. Asserting authority through appearance and formality. We were faced with the mirage of competence at every turn.

Sangna, our French gendarmes, Jamie (the future Harvard man), and I stepped out into the heat and made our way up the dusty remnants of a pathway towards the district police station. I felt anxious about the response that awaited us and apprehensive about how useful the investigation would now be.

The first sounds of sleeping men reached us as we entered the station. In hammocks slung inside the first room we entered, four men slept and snored. I looked at Sangna, who was busy nodding and smiling.

"They are sleeping," he said to me when he saw that I was looking to him for explanation.

"Yes," I said.

"It is too hot," he said. "So they sleep."

"Police," I said, slightly bewildered.

"Police," he said and smiled. "We should come back." He yawned at me. "Sorry, sir," he said through the yawn.

Discarded sandals and lime-green uniforms lay under each swaying hammock. As I stood watching them and not knowing what to do next, I felt a deep longing to be in one of the hammocks. My eyelids ached to close.

When they finally awoke they nodded to us and, through Sangna, asked us to wait outside.

The slow-motion movement of the culture caused us endless frustrations. We set deadlines, had expectations, and expected progress. The Peace Accord was designed to allow for an eighteen-month period in which to establish democratic institutions, such as courts, hold free and fair elections, build roads, and feed everyone. As unrealistic as the Accord was, the world could literally not afford more time for a mission that would cost billions. The fallacy of these timelines first became evident to me on that sweltering day on the veranda of a police station as we waited for the men inside to dress. The heat slowed everyone down, and would certainly have an impact on the ambitious timelines of the Peace Accord.

The commander of the station came out to us in his crisp uniform and Bavarian-style police hat and smiled. "Hello," he said in English. And everything I imagined of this meeting proved wrong. He was friendly and relaxed and open and helpful to us, and in his sleeping sarong when we met him in his hammock, hardly overdressed.

Then, more of the unexpected. As we sat down on a bamboo bench set off in a corner of the office and as he pulled out his handwritten notes of the police investigation so far, my eyes glanced along a wall of photographs. Most were of Cambodian dignitaries—Hun Sen, Prince Sihanouk—and of UN dignitaries and foreign ambassadors. The wall seemed to be some kind of honour wall, an attempt, it occurred to me, to elevate the prestige of the dusty police station by tacking celebrities' pictures to a wall. But I began to notice other photographs as part of the mix, of distant images of lone men walking or in small groups, of men I did not recognize, both Asian and Occidental. Some of the pictures were grainy and taken from a distance, others closer but equally blurry. The photos seemed to have been taken quickly or from some concealed position. As I carelessly scanned the entire bank of images in front of us, I recognized something familiar in one of the shots. How could it be? I thought, as I focused on the one that had caught my attention. I could hardly believe what I was looking at, and at what stared back at me. There, on the wall, amidst an array of faces, was my own, glistening with sweat and deep in conversation with my boss, Denis McNamara. My photograph had been taken some weeks before, when I had first arrived in the country. The cameraman was a fair distance from me when he snapped and the picture was slightly out of focus and crooked. But there was no doubt who it was. This grainy image of my upper body on that wall seemed profoundly disturbing to me at that moment. I was about to begin the UN's first formal murder investigation in a remote and previously isolated rural Cambodia with the eyes of nervous stakeholders watching and there I was, on a wall. I certainly was not a dignitary, warranting honour in such a place as this. Then why?

It took me some time to work it out in my mind and to shake loose my life experiences to date. We were in a society in which enemies and potential enemies were closely monitored, followed, watched, photographed. This was new for me. I was one of the first UN human rights investigators in the country and my boss was the director of the human rights component of the mission. Human rights were the great judgemental benchmark of the decade and we were their police. Donor governments would read our reports first for hints of a crumbling Peace Accord. So in the eyes of the government, we had to be monitored.

The police commander saw my expression and turned to follow my stare to the picture on his wall. He immediately seemed to blush and then pointed to my arm and spoke. Sangna looked at my arm and said, "He asks you what happened to your watch." In the photograph on his wall I wore a watch, a watch that I had lost some days before.

"Lost," I said.

His face serious, he said, "Too bad."

Cambodia had been isolated from the West for over a decade. That isolation had been at the instigation of the United States and implemented by the United Nations. Cambodians had good reason to be wary of us. So I, like most others in the early days of the UN mission, was being followed. I immediately began privately recounting my nightly explorations of Phnom Penh. Had they watched me at the hotel bar or the press club or Hotel Cambodiana where we gathered?

The hotel bar. If they had followed me on a night that past week, they would have thought me a fool and a danger to no one but myself. On that night, I had gone out into the Cambodian night seeking adventure.

Adventure began with a drink at my hotel, the Hotel Le Royal, and its exuberant bar scene. Expats gathered there in packs to drink and enjoy electricity. "The lights are working here. Wahh. They will pay a fortune for this," I overheard a member of one of the French non-governmental organizations (NGOs) say. They all seemed preoccupied with power and lights going on and off.

Sitting at the bar, I had ordered a Tiger beer. The hotel was in the grand style of French opulent colonialism. Big, wide corridors. Banistered winding staircase to the top floor with a large skylight at the apex. Twenty-foot ceilings. Balconies off each room. Two-person cage elevator. Clawfoot bathtubs. Pool and cottages out back. It was not hard to imagine officials of the French Expeditionary Force of 1929 in their pith helmets and dress whites striding in and out of the hotel holding the arm of a woman in a large hat. With a free hand she'd be madly waving a fan the size of her hat, having just disembarked from a *cyclopouse*, a bicycle-type rickshaw taxi driven by a coolie. Today, the elevator doesn't work, greenish-brown water dribbles into the bathtub, and bats and monkeys share quarters in the top floor. The coolies are still waiting by their cyclos outside the gates, however, and, I am sure, still asking the same question they asked 100 years before: "*Voulez-vous une fille, monsieur?*" One had asked me. "*Non?*" He replied to my hesitations. He was a bronzed man in torn clothes with sinewy legs and blackened and missing teeth from the betel nut he incessantly chewed. With a slightly crooked gaping smile he added, "*Garçon?*"

Foreign journalists said that agents of the Khmer Rouge posed as cyclo-pouse drivers to infiltrate the city. The ones I met were mostly pimps.

"Yer UN, are ya?" I heard the familiar drawl of an Australian. Australian disdain for the British, "wincing poms," they call them, is reflected in their use of the English language. They resist fully forming their mouths around vowels, I discovered, as if to protest association to their cousins, the wincing poms.

I turned to the voice and saw a dark-haired woman sitting at the end of the bar, sleeves on her khaki shirt rolled up almost to her shoulders, glaring at me over her Tiger beer. She was tall, slim, muscular, and deeply tanned. She looked as if she had been working in a rice paddy all day.

"Yes," I answered, "I guess I am."

"Well, try not to fuck up the country too much." A murmur of laughter circled the bar.

"Thanks for the tip," I said. "Cheers." I raised my beer to her and tried to smile.

"Ah. Don't go crying on me. Just yankin' yer chain." she said, "Liz Franklin." She raised her glass of beer and ice and took a long drink. The warnings I had had about ice and botulism rang empty to me when warm beer was served up in a forty-plus climate. I tonged the ice into my glass and then poured in the foaming beer and drank with relish. Frosty-cold, watery beer.

Liz was a civil engineer from Canberra working in Cambodia for an organization called Save the Children, Australia, an NGO. She ran their field projects in the countryside, from well drilling to something called the cow bank, a mechanism allowing farmers to borrow animals from a centralized bank of cows and use them to plow and fertilize fields.

"We can get those damn cows into the bank no probs," she told me.

"But getting them out of instant tellers, now that's a challenge." It was her great joke and the fact of telling it to me was her gift. The NGO community was known for their strident devotion to work and their humourless lives. They resented the UN largely because it had done little or nothing for Cambodia in its years of anguish after Pol Pot fell. The NGOs had taken up the humanitarian slack. Poorly paid, highly motivated zealots descended. Liz was one, but at least she could laugh.

Liz was sharply critical of the peace accord that was bringing the UN into the country and ending a decade-long conflict. It would bring corruption, chaos, and the return to power of a king, she told me. She knew Hun Sen, the president, and Sihanouk, the prince-to-be-king-again. Her opinion of Hun Sen was that he was the man of destiny for Cambodia, an intelligent modernist who had been a Khmer Rouge cadre and defected to stay alive. She called Sihanouk a buffoon, a man of butter, for his taste for all things French. He worried her most.

I was captivated by her acquaintance with these pivotal characters and other actors on this bizarro stage. Khieu Sampan, the acting figurehead of the Khmer Rouge, she had known from the border camps, where she had once worked. Pol Pot himself she had never seen. She had met his wife, she told me. "She was chained to a tree," she said. "Mad as my aunt Margaret. She was the brains, you know. She was the one." Liz was referring to the theory that Pol Pot's wife and her twin sister had been the masterminds of their coming to power and for the travesty that followed. "Tough old bird."

We talked through the smoke and ice beer and heat for another hour, and then she said, "Let's go to my place." So we did.

Naked and drenched in our mingled sweat, Liz suddenly put her hand up and said, "Condom or diaphragm?" like she was a waitress asking if I wanted soup or salad. With my eyes stinging from the salt water we were swimming in, I squeezed them dry and said, "Condom." She nodded—was it approval?—and reached behind her. "What size?" I expected her to ask. But she didn't. I put the little helmet on, we had the slipperiest sex I've had, and then I thought of the curfew.

"Jesus Christ," I blurted out.

"What?" She was on her stomach, back and bum glistening.

"I have to go. There is a curfew," I said, groping in the dark for my underwear and expecting a protest. Sex never came easy, in my experience. I would be expected to cuddle and have a talk and stay till morning.

"Gawd. Green as they come.... Go," she said, and then seemed to fall asleep.

Feeling slightly hurt by the ease of the dismissal, I found clothes, dressed, and walked out into a pitch-black Cambodian night.

Phnom Penh had been emptied by Pol Pot in 1975. A million or more inhabitants were force-marched into the countryside in Cambodia's Great Leap Forward. It was a leap into an abyss of starvation, murder, and ruin. The numbers of those killed between 1975 and 1979 during the Khmer Rouge era are hard to pinpoint. Propaganda and no census obscure the truth. Two million are said by the Cambodian government to have been exterminated by Pol Pot. *Two million.* The true figure is anyone's guess, with figures ranging from 700,000 to 1.7 million. Many, if not more than half of those who died during the Pol Pot era, died from starvation in a centrally planned economic and agricultural disaster. Politicals and other enemies were indeed murdered, but probably not in the millions. The vast majority of Pol Pot's killings were the result of criminal negligence, not homicide.

The Vietnamese entered Cambodia in December 1978 and the killings and starvation ended. In 1979 the US continued to carry a heavy grudge for their loss in the Indo-Chinese War. At every opportunity, in each political arena, they pounded their grudge with the alacrity of Khrushchev's shoe. An embargo on Cambodia—then called Kampuchea—and Vietnam was imposed, and military and other aid ferried to the rebels along the border. One such rebel group that benefited from this Western intervention was the Khmer Rouge, which had fled into border territories after being initially vanquished by the Vietnamese army. To punish the Vietnamese, the US policy on Cambodia allowed the Khmer Rouge to flourish.

Americans will do anything, anything at all, if they hate your guts.

But they were fun to play with. At international donor group meetings or other mini United Nations sessions in Bangkok, our office prepared the groundwork by arranging the seating, passing out materials, writing speeches. I did all this. The countries were arranged in alphabetical seating. The United States preceded Vietnam in the alphabetized country seating plan. I laid out the name cards. We were instructed not to sit the US delegate beside the Vietnamese. The US had requested it, I was told.

So, of course, the first chance I had, I sat them right beside each other off in a corner, like two pals. The delegates began arriving. The Americans arrived in dark suits and scowls. They saw where they were sitting. The tall, tanned, and fit-looking American looked over at the empty Vietnamese chairs and appeared to be sniffing them. In the end the Vietnamese didn't come.

In 1992, with a fierce embargo in the process of finally ending and a war just over, Phnom Penh was grim and bare. Roads went unrepaired, electricity was scarce, drinking water brown or green. Guerrillas lay hidden and dormant in the city. Criminals were becoming bolder and more desperate. In the back streets of this city, the city that grew more and more dangerous by the hour, in the black of a moonless, lampless night, I stepped out of Liz's house and onto her balcony. At that moment, I had never felt more content. Still damp with sweat, I heard stirrings of a breeze in the palms and paused on the balcony to savour it. The coolness of that air wrapped around my body and fluttered through my open shirt. I recognized that moment as precious. My worldly possessions were contained in two duffle bags. I had no one to answer to. I had enough money to live. I was working for the UN in a place that seemed to need us. I had just had sex. I could move, change jobs, remake myself countless times. I was buoyant and happy and invincible.

In the distance, the clacking of a rice seller's batons was the only sound I heard. It was the music of the Phnom Penh night. Nothing else. No one else. The night was clear and ablaze with stars. No city lights impeded, no pollution obscured. I was standing at a portal to the heavens. My portal.

I finally descended from Liz's balcony and strolled over to my Land Cruiser, with its leather interior and air conditioning, pushed into the tape deck the only cassette in the vehicle, the soundtrack from Disney's *The Little Mermaid*, and backed onto the street, a lane of deep mud. As the wheels spun and then grabbed hold, the Land Cruiser swerved slightly, then gripped and began moving forward. I felt supremely confident at that moment. I was driving a vehicle I could never afford to buy at home. I was in the dangerous backstreets of the city Pol Pot emptied in 1975, and I had just manoeuvred my truck out of the mud, the same mud Vietnamese troops had chased the Khmer Rouge through. With headlights on high beam I turned left at the first intersection, then right at the next. Sebastian, the Little Mermaid's crab advisor, was singing "Under the Sea" in his Caribbean calypso voice.

Two more turns and the vehicle swerved hard as I gunned it just to feel the skid and the pleasure of controlling the skid. Once the fishtail had subsided and I was headed straight again, I eased on the brakes and finally brought the Land Cruiser to a stop. The road ahead seemed to end at a large mound of earth. The right turn led into a wall of crumbling bricks. On the left was swamp. I sat and looked and knew that I was lost. I hadn't bothered to remember the turns from Liz's house as I drove away, feeling as I did—so confident, so sated. I didn't have a clue where the hotel was. No street signs marked the way at corners. The crab was singing, "Even the slug here, cutting the rug, here ... under the sea...." I plucked out the tape and sat for long minutes feeling something new. A slight panic was welling in me.

Looking out the windows and deep into the shadows, I saw cyclo-driver sleeper agents of Pol Pot's army watching me with their yellow eyes. I had money, a nice car, and white skin. My ample skin would look good on Pol Pot's wall. I put the car into reverse and backed up.

I struggled to see the road behind in the faint luminescence of the red taillights. It was like looking into a cave with a match. How close was I to the swamp on my right, or was it my left? The road seemed to branch right, with space enough for me to back into and turn around. I was rotating the steering wheel left to make the manoeuvre and trying to ease backward when my foot slipped on the accelerator and the vehicle jumped back and suddenly dipped down and to the left. I slammed the clutch and brake pedal and cranked up the emergency brake. The vehicle stopped but seemed to be teetering over the edge of something. It must be the swamp, I thought. "Shit," I said out loud.

I sat for a moment and tried to think. I knew that in driving forward I would need to release the brakes and risk slipping further into the swamp— perhaps irretrievably so. I decided to get out and have a look, see how precarious the balance was.

I opened the door and swung my legs out and into a mud that immediately oozed up and over my ankles. Plopping through it I made my way to the rear for a look. The back left wheel was part way down a small culvert built to carry running water and probably sewage from a house. Not a vast boundless pit. I was confident that the Land Cruiser would not slide easily down into it when I shifted into first and released the brakes. Relieved, I turned to retrace my footsteps and get back into the Land Cruiser when I was startled by the image of what appeared to be a woman standing across the road. She was as still and silent as a statue and she was looking right at me. What was she doing there, in the mud, in the dark empty street long after curfew? Unsettled by the odd sight, I tried projecting an easy casualness, so I waved to her as I moved to the open door of the Land Cruiser. She didn't return the gesture. I concluded that she was merely a curious resident of the street out to see a *barang* (Khmer slang for European foreigner) stuck in mud. Our white skin and long noses were so unusual for locals that they would sometimes freeze in fascination and stare with mouths agape.

"Beautiful night," I called to the statue across the street of mud.

Activated by the sound of my voice, she immediately started in motion and began crossing the road towards me. As she approached I could see that she wore a long one-piece floral dress and had tied her hair up in a bun. Her face seemed to be painted white, with red circles of rouge on her cheeks, like a clown's mask. I stopped to watch her, frozen by the utter strangeness of her. What is this? I thought.

With a speed and purpose of movement that caught me completely off guard, she began running straight at me and before I could break from the trance I was in, she had closed the gap between us, managing to wedge into the space between where I stood and the door to the Land Cruiser. Her face, I could now see, was powdered a thick, heavy white, and was streaked and blotched with what looked like sweat and smeared rouge from her cheeks. Black circles had been penciled around both eyes.

"Excuse me," I said and tried to go around her. Stepping out to block my way, she pushed firmly into me, forcing me against the back door. She was strong, too strong. I looked closer. Khmer features in men and women are smaller than those of Occidentals and often are indiscernible as between the sexes. But for a woman, this person's ears, nose, and chin protruded too much. A large hand clutched at a plastic bag. She was a man, I realized, a man in woman's clothing, something I had not yet seen in Cambodia. In addition to the white makeup and the rouge, she had big, red lips and smelled heavily of a pungent, nauseating perfume. With her free hand she grabbed for my crotch. I pushed her hand aside. "Please," I said. "Go away."

Licking her lips fervently in what I took to be some kind of suggestive sexual gesture she began repeating one word over and over, "Ic'ream. Ic'ream." She pawed at my pants.

"No!" I said pushing her.

"Ic'ream! Ic'ream!" she insisted and then motioned back and forth from and to her open mouth with her hand slightly cupped. She was mimicking fellatio. "No!" I said and tried to push past her. Her physical aggression surprised me and I could not easily dislodge her. I could smell alcohol and smoke and rich garlic on her breath. In desperation, I reached into my pocket and took out a wad of riel notes. "Here," I said, shoving them at her, "take these." I gave her all I had, a thick packet of Cambodian money. She took the offering and immediately stepped away. I didn't hesitate. Climbing into the vehicle, my heart racing, I closed the door, started the engine and drove. Mud kicked up from the back wheels as I put my foot down. The Land Cruiser twisted and slid sideways and finally was moving. I looked at where she had been, but she was gone, back into the night, a little richer.

I was shaken by what had happened. I had to be more careful in this city, at least until I understood its hidden dangers. The war had been prolonged and bloody, and the poverty had been prolonged and poisonous. There were demons out there. And not just those of Pol Pot's making.

I would come to see in Cambodia, and later in Tajikistan, how a people can be left bruised by war and depravation. Violent images, fear, want, combine to affect a people at the deepest levels. Social interactions are different against this backdrop. Conversations are muted and dark. Everything has an extra touch of aggression in its makeup. Even laughter. Arguments flare. Accidents end in shootings. Quarrels end in murder. These are bruises that reflect the cheapening of life. Its devaluation had grown, day by day, killing by killing, until the survivors or witnesses or even the killers had absorbed all they could bear and then became not immune—never immune—but inert. Dead inside watching the dead outside.

I had just witnessed a desperate and hungry transvestite come out of the night to offer me sex for money, communicating with the only words she knew in English—*ice cream*.

As I wound my way through the badly pitted, muddy roads and finally found the main street of the city and the route to my hotel, I had a sense that for a fleeting moment I had brushed against what lay outside the hotel compounds and below the running boards of Land Cruisers. There was fear and desperation out there. I best always have enough money to buy my freedom from it.

Days following that encounter in the back streets of Phnom Penh, I sat looking up at my photograph on the district police station wall, thinking that my encounter with Ms. Ic'ream had been observed by security agents who undoubtedly went off with peals of laughter and certainly retold the story when they gave my picture to the police commander. Here is one you need have no fear of, they must have said.

The police commander was smiling at me as he relayed to me his report of their investigation of the killings. It is always more enjoyable when your opponent is an idiot.

The report was simple. The protesters were angry, he told me, over land they thought was theirs. They closed the road and marched and chanted and had been headed for the headman's house.

"Why him?" I asked.

He had been accused by the people of stealing their land and failing to compensate them, as they had been promised. The police formed a line in the road and fired into the air. They had not shot into the crowd, he said. They were not barbarians. They wanted to frighten the people, no more, he said. When the shooting stopped, two lay dead on the road. The commander said that they had not been killed by police. My American colleague Jamie and I nodded and listened and did not believe a word he said. I took notes in a black notebook, splashed with drops of my own sweat.

We thanked him and refused his offer of a police escort into the village. Then we were back in the Land Cruiser and the cool air and were heading for the village and what we hoped would be the truth of what happened that night.

Standing on the road over a patch of dried blood surrounded by children, most of whom were hopping on one leg and laughing at me, I wondered what to do next. The gendarmes stood off to one side in their powder blue, with their confused expressions. Jamie was staring into the blood stain. Sangna smoked.

"Ask the children," I finally said to Sangna. "Ask them who shot the protestors."

Sangna called to a few of the older boys and then crouched down to their level. I saw him speak to them. I saw their arms rise together and point, off the road and into the trees along the road.

"The shots came from here," Sangna called to me, pointing as the children had. "From the trees ... not the police."

We walked off the road and into the bush and trees. A small hut with a woman selling drinks stood a few metres from the road. "Ask her, Sangna, ask her about the shooting."

Sangna spoke to her and she shook her and head and gestured to her hut. "They shot through her hut," he said. "Look, the marks of shooting." Sangna was pointing at chips and scars and holes in the side of the drink lady's hut, marks caused by bullets.

"So, not the line of police on the road. But, who...?"

Through the course of the day we came to learn how the village headman and his sons, long since escaped from the area, had opened fire from the forest by the side of the road on the hapless group of protesters. The headman had stolen their land and had failed to pay compensation. Knowing that the UN was arriving to Cambodia, the villagers had felt emboldened and daring and had decided to seek justice for the first time in their lives. They were marching down the road to confront the headman and take the land back. Land was a precious commodity and becoming ever more precious with a quarter of a million refugees poised to return from camps along the borders. What we had uncovered through the course of the investigation was a lesson in Third World politics and human rights work that I would not soon forget. Follow the land, always follow the land, and there you will find the root of your conflict, and often the identity of your killer.

THEY KILLED CHILDREN

(Chong Khneas, Lake Tonle Sap, Cambodia—March 1993)

There came a moment for me in Cambodia when I began to understand the impulse for blind, unbridled revenge and thought, in that instant, of how good intentions could turn to war.

In the floating village of Chong Khneas on Lake Tonle Sap in northeastern Cambodia an attack had occurred. Rows of dead children lay in small wooden caskets, and in the local hospital a dying baby panted through his pain with a bullet lodged, unbelievably, in his testicles. We raced away from the village in a Zodiac rubber dingy, a British Military Observer (MILOB) at the controls, heading southeast, along the coast, knowing that the attackers had followed that very route in long wooden boats with slow, quiet engines. They had left one of their numbers behind, killed by a defender's lucky shot in the dark. I saw his gas-bloated body floating like a pool toy, his swollen wrist tied to the dock by a rope the size of a shoelace, his humanity gone.

"We have to be cautious," the MILOB shouted back through the wind to us. "The Khmer Rouge have told us that we cannot be on this part of the lake. Not welcome...."

We had little doubt about the identity of the killers, as the politics of an

attack on a Vietnamese village seemed clear enough. But if we were to accuse the Khmer Rouge leadership of such an atrocity, we had to be more
certain. So we pounded over the water, on the trail of murderers.

The anger and desire to do harm to those who had committed such atrocities was overwhelming me. The faces of dead children. A baby gasping in
his death throes. Mothers collapsed on the dock and fathers hammering
away at caskets—hard release with a hammer. The impulse in me was strong
and visceral. This was all too real.

For weeks we had heard this coming, this attack on innocents, but had
not understood what it meant. The Khmer Rouge radio station had begun
broadcasting the vilest propaganda aimed at inciting racial hatred. Target-
ing the Vietnamese living in Cambodia, the broadcasts played on the Cambodian fear and mistrust of everything Vietnamese. The hatred of them. The
fear of them. Pol Pot's lies.

Fourteen-month-old Lim Sou, wide-eyed, dying. "We cannot help him,"
the doctors told me. "Too much infection." How did that bullet find its
way to this most vulnerable place? My interpreter Kiempo answered, "Kru
Khmer magic," he said. "Evil."

Up to that point, religious faith had been a constant, though subtle, presence in my life, a gentle hand on my shoulder, rather than a firm grip on my
arm. My experiences in the UN began to erode my faith and push that hand
away. I could not reconcile the notion of a loving God with the suffering
of innocents that I witnessed. Finally, it was while watching that baby, and
listening to the cries of his aunt sitting nearby, that I felt the last finger of
God's hand on my life begin to slip away.

The Khmer Rouge radio broadcasts had spewed lies that the Vietnamese
had infiltrated into Cambodia to conquer and dominate. Soldiers, it was
claimed, had been planted by retreating armies to assimilate the Khmer, to
marry and breed and destroy the Khmer. The message had been heard, it had
been understood, and it had been believed. Tell a lie often enough, call it the
truth, and you will convince a captive audience, one that wants to believe,
one that lives in the jungle and is hardened and sour with primitive sorrows.
Malaria. Hunger. Death. The *Youn* (Khmer derogatory slang for Vietnamese)
were to blame for all Cambodia's miseries, ordinary Cambodians had come
to believe.

We were approaching a village that sat over the water on wooden stilts, built when the lake was shallow. These were permanent homes, not like the floating villages of the Vietnamese that could pick up and move to follow the fish. Rows of houses, water streets, boat taxis. The Zodiac slowed.

The British MILOB said, "This is dicey. We may not be able to see if any Khmer soldiers are nearby. The huts block our view. We need to find out."

A boat with a lone fisherman, net extended over the bow, came chugging out of the village, headed for the centre of the lake. "Here we go," said the MILOB. "Let's ask him." He gunned the Zodiac and headed straight for it.

We closed the gap between the crafts in seconds.

The fisherman didn't seem surprised by our appearance. His face was stained a deep brown, almost black, and leathered with criss-cross furrows from long days on open water under a South Asian sun. He looked up at us and smiled, showing us his toothless, watery gums. Kiempo engaged him in conversation and in a moment we had our answer.

"They are not here, sir," said Kiempo, translating. "They came last night and took boats. They returned them. They are from a unit that stays a small way inland, over that slope." Kiempo pointed to the landside. "He says they come often to trade. Sometimes to take." Kiempo and the fisherman laughed.

"Was it them, did they attack the Vietnamese?"

"He does not know." Which meant, he did not care. They were *Youn*, after all.

The Zodiac spun away and headed toward the Cambodian village.

We stopped at the first hut at which we could see people. Our interpreter asked, "Can we speak with you, about the Khmer Rouge...? Why not?"

The answer finally came back that the villagers were not afraid of the Khmer Rouge, that they were invited patriots, coming for food and boats and paying, always. They were always polite, cordial, and honest, we were told; admired by the young men for purity, respected by the elders for honesty. It made me ill to hear them praised.

"They killed children," I said to the man of the hut, squatting on our haunches in his hut, sipping the green tea served by his daughters.

"I do not know," he answered me.

"Up the lake, a dozen or so, killed."

The man sat in silence and then refused to answer any other questions. The Khmer Rouge were protecting this village, we came to learn. Allegiance and boats were the price for their protection. Oh, and sons. They came for their sons.

IT IS TOO BIG FOR HIM

(Phnom Penh, Cambodia—January, 1993)

During its reign of terror, the Khmer Rouge had killed or chased the judges away. When the Khmer Rouge was ousted, Hun Sen's regime allowed courts to function, but ensured that the judges remained under tight control. I saw this first-hand, following the arrest of a police officer for the murder of a member of the political opposition.

As the election approached in Cambodia, and the opposition organized and grew bold, the unthinkable began to happen. On a daily basis, under the watchful eye of one of the largest and most expensive operations in the United Nations' history, members of the political parties in opposition to the government of Hun Sen began to die. Machine-gunnings, grenade attacks, pistol shots, claymore explosions—political murder became a daily event. The government denied responsibility, blaming criminals or personal vendettas as the cause of the river of blood that now appeared. I saw my first dead body. I saw my first dead child. I saw my first 100 dead bodies. The United Nations stood by, guns well-oiled and silent. The UN leadership in New York and in Cambodia wished on falling stars that the killing would stop, the election happen, and we all return home with laurels. At first they repeated what Hun Sen's gang had told them at their tea parties: that we should not confuse death, in a land of murder, with politics. The UN Special Representative in Cambodia initially repeated this mantra because he wanted so badly to believe it. But in the field, standing close beside the opposition parties, and the corpses, the human rights workers knew differently. We talked to the people, we went to the kill sites, we picked up the shell casings, we followed the shoot lines, we did the ballistics tests, we took the statements, and most of all, we listened to the politics. Basil Fernando, a human rights lawyer from Sri Lanka and the UN Human Rights Legal Director, himself a victim of political violence, knew it the minute the killings began. We started a list of killings: two, eight, ten, fifteen, twenty.... They could not be ignored. A UN special task force to investigate the killings was finally formed and the powers of arrest delegated to UN police officers. A UN special prosecutor was appointed with the mandate to issue warrants and summonses and to prosecute cases in the Cambodian courts. It was bold and it was desperate, and it came about because nothing else worked and the spectre of failure loomed.

I was the human rights lawyer assigned to the task force, which included a rotation of Irish homicide detectives and Malaysian and Australian police. Once assembled, the task force waited for the right killing to take place, a killing that would allow us to flex our new powers and to act decisively. As it turned out, we didn't have to wait long.

As we were about to leave our office in Phnom Penh one night, the call from Kampot province came in. On the line was the human rights officer we had stationed there, a picket to alert us of a fresh kill. "We have one," she said. "We have taken a policeman ... for killing a Funcinpec man." Funcinpec was a political party running against Hun Sen and was his most formidable threat. The party was well-organized, financed by the Americans and led by princeling Norodom Ranariddh, the son of Prince Sihanouk and associated with the prince himself. With Sihanouk's princely dust on their shoulders, they were indeed a threat to Hun Sen. Consequently, most of those being killed were from the Funcinpec party.

"Where is he now?" I asked quickly over the line, expecting it to cut off at any moment.

"We gave him to the local police, handed him over. The French military arrested him and then handed him over. What else could they do?"

She was right, we were not yet in a position to hold prisoners. But now time was against us. We had to get to the police station in Kampot before this man disappeared. "What happened?" I asked her.

The night before, a group of men came to the Funcinpec man's hut, located in a field in Kampot province, located approximately 150 kilometres from Phnom Penh. It was dark and the man was alone with his wife and twelve-year-old daughter. The killers chased him out of the hut, then shot him dead. His wife grabbed the girl and they ran for their lives. She clutched at that little girl, almost half her size, and sprinted over uneven, rocky ground. The killers could not see her in the dark, but heard her breathing and her heavy footfalls. They fired in her direction and missed. They threw grenades at her and missed. When I arrived the next day I saw the craters, three in a row, from the grenades thrown at that woman.

She then hid in a line of bush some 500 metres away and was found the next morning by French paratroopers patrolling the zone. She could not walk, nor could she for weeks afterward. She had shredded the muscles in her calves and thighs in her sprint to save her daughter and herself. The paratroopers found her curled over her daughter, protecting her from everyone. They had to pry her off. She fought them at first, I was told, until they convinced her they meant no harm. The French found the body of her husband and then radioed for the local police. The woman was sitting by the hut when the police arrived. "It is him," the mother said, pointing to one of the government police officers. "He was here last night. He killed my husband." A French soldier grabbed the man that instant. "Sure?" said the French. "Sure," said the mother.

Held in the UN compound for several hours, the man was eventually handed over to the local police until the UN decided what next to do.

We arrived by helicopter to make that decision.

I listened as the UN detectives interviewed the mother, the lone witness to the killing. "How could you see in the dark? How could you be sure it was him?"

"I know him," she told the detectives. "I know his voice. Another had a torch. I saw his profile. It is him."

With reasonable grounds to make an arrest, we then approached the provincial Communist Party committee and the police. A meeting was quickly arranged. I thanked the committee for convening, and extolled the value of such co-operation in these perilous times. I commended the police for holding the prisoner for us. I told them that he would receive a fair trial in Phnom Penh, that we would ensure him a lawyer.

The head of the delegation of a dozen or so committee members replied that there had been a misunderstanding, that the officer in their custody had been on duty at the time of the killing and was seen in the police station at that time. He then explained that because of the genocidal rule of Pol Pot, their resources were depleted and police officers worked long shifts. He was working such a shift.

I thanked him for the information and assured him that evidence collected by their police would form part of the record that would go before a judge. Our detectives had concluded that enough evidence existed for a judge to hear it, however. We would be taking him in.

"Thank you," he said, "for bringing UN police to assist in their investigation but the UN has no jurisdiction in this matter and it will be handled locally. If the UN wants to share its findings with our investigators, that would be given due consideration."

For two-and-one-half hours the discussion, the negotiation, continued. I was told of the excesses of Pol Pot, of the difficulties the government now faced, of the jurisdiction of their court. I countered with explanations of the Peace Accord and the UN's overall supervisory role in the administration of justice. We then took a break in our discussions.

Outside, a circle of UN police and military stood around me, both from the task force and the local unit in that area.

"Listen," I said. "I need to tell the Cambodians that we are prepared to enter the police station by force and take the prisoner if we have to."

"You're crazy," said a French military officer.

"I don't intend on doing it. I merely will tell them this. We have a heavily armed French brigade here. These people don't know what we are capable of. Please, just support me on this."

Amid a rising cloud of cigarette smoke, we found consensus to support my bluff and we returned to the negotiations.

"Thank you for listening to us," I began after we were seated, "but it is getting late and our helicopter is scheduled to return soon. I am afraid that we must take this man back with us to Phnom Penh. We have our orders.

We will proceed to the jail and take him. I ask you now, will your people give him to us or resist?"

Only one of the officials opposite me had been engaged in the discussions. The others silently watched and listened for the translations and their negotiator's responses. When my words finally were translated to the negotiator he bent his head to whisper to the man beside. He then looked at me and smiled.

I felt a rivulet of sweat making its way down the side of my face. My throat was parched dry from the tension of the moment. I reached for a bottle of water on the table and took a quick sip.

He held on to that smile, as if in breaking it he would plunge us both further than we dared go.

"You have no jurisdiction," he finally said. "You will break our law."

"I believe I do," I answered, sensing his hesitancy. "The Peace Accord gives it to me. The French military is outside. We will go to the prison. What is your answer? Will you resist?"

He paused and looked to his comrades for support. "We will discuss this," he stated, and with that he rose and left the room.

"You're crazy," the French said to me. "We can't attack these people."

Lost in the moment and the heat and the dryness of my mouth, I had pushed too hard. Without the military's commitment to back me up, I had pledged the use of force as a heavy-handed response to recalcitrance. I was out on a limb, and my French partners in enforcement wanted no part of this dangerous tactic.

The Cambodians returned to the room and took their seats. The man I had been negotiating with was no longer present, his seat left vacant across from me. Another man spoke, one I had not noticed before and who had been silent throughout. His voice was strong and authoritative. I instantly was of the impression that he was the leader all along and only now had come forward. He turned his chair so that he looked out the window as he spoke, never once looking at me. He was angry.

"Do you take the same position?" he asked. "If we do not release him to you. What will you do?"

This was my chance to back down, he was giving me a way out. I didn't take it, I had gone too far already.

"With regret, we will go with force to the police station and take our prisoner." My heart beat lumps down the side of my neck.

He stared out the window, turned in his chair and then stood. "You can have him," he finally said.

A paper was drawn for the prisoner's release to me and we shook hands and left the room. With perfect Hollywood timing, our helicopter from Phnom Penh banked low into view and came clattering down in clouds of dust in the UN compound across the road.

We had arrested a police officer in his own country for the murder of a political opponent of his government. A first for us, and a turning point.

"Well done," one of the Irish police said as he sidled up to me. "You've done this before."

I had done nothing like it in my life. Ever.

"Here," he said handing me a water bottle.

I took it and drank deeply, filling my bone-dry mouth and letting the water flow over my parched lips.

I slept in the helicopter on the way back to Phnom Penh, the thump, thump, thump of the rotors a gentle pat on the back, soothing me to sleep. Our prisoner sat with us, plastic handcuffs on his wrists. I dreamt on the flight that a spider was eating my leg.

Once in Phnom Penh we attempted for hours to find a UN military or police unit that would hold our prisoner. No one would take him. No one had been notified. No one had been ordered. It was then past 8 p.m. and we sat with our prisoner in the back of a Land Cruiser on a side street in the capital, wondering if we should take him home, tuck him into bed.

The operation had happened too quickly after the implementation of the new directives on UN corrective human rights action. Memos had not been circulated throughout the country, and, as we came to learn, the UN leadership never believed this kind of direct action would actually be taken. They still lived in hope that Hun Sen was being truthful and that his police and army were not killing the political opposition. But in our back seat, relaxed and seemingly content to be on this trip to Phnom Penh at our expense, one of the political killers sat as living proof.

We finally managed to track down the UN civilian police commander, who reluctantly agreed to order one of his police units to take the prisoner for the night, which they reluctantly did.

The next morning, as was required by the criminal law, we brought the prisoner before the Phnom Penh court.

The Phnom Penh Central Court resembled a squalid block of slum in any inner city. Broken windows, unkempt property, cracked concrete walls. Missing doors. Inside the smell of must and mould. Surrounded by mud year round, even in the dry season, the inside bore muddied footprints of everyone who entered.

The UN special prosecutor, the legal director of the human rights unit, and I met for over an hour with a judge of the court. The law on detention was newly promulgated and minimally disseminated within the courts. We carried a translated copy with us for the judge. We took him through each section, explaining the rights of the accused and the need for an order from a judge to detain before we could keep him any longer.

The judge sat politely listening to everything we had to say about the arrest, the law, and the grounds for detention. As our prosecutor spoke I watched a pair of geckos twirling their marble eyes at us from a vertical hold on the adjacent wall. Absolutely still except for those magic eyes, they were also waiting, it seemed, for the judge to make his decision.

The questions the judge asked were intelligent and insightful. He wanted to know the grounds upon which he could order the detention and the standard of evidence we had to demonstrate. He queried the accused's right to counsel at this stage as well as his own jurisdiction, given that the arrest had taken place in a different province in Cambodia. Nodding vigorously, he then stood and said he would consider how to proceed. Could we wait? Of course, we said, take your time.

It began to rain outside in the typical fashion of Cambodia. A torrential downpour from nowhere that slapped down hard onto the giant palm leaves outside our open window.

"That went well," the prosecutor said. "He has a lot to think about."

The legal director, Basil Fernando, knew from his own experience the stresses on judges and lawyers in a system of heavy-handed and delinquent police. Himself the subject of a police-orchestrated assassination plot, Basil had fled Sri Lanka, his pregnant wife, and his life's work, after being tipped off by allies within the police force itself.

"What do you think, Basil?" I asked him.

He emitted a loud "Hmmm," as was his habit, and rubbed his chin. "You see," he said almost shouting at us, a pattern of speech we had grown familiar with, though no more comfortable. "This judge is faced with a dilemma now. He must act on his own, without a government member or police officer telling him what they want him to do. Hopefully, the phones in here are not working. Do they have phones?"

"Why?" I asked.

"So he cannot confer with anyone. He will be told not to do what we ask, I'm sure. It will be a reflex, for him. A judge cannot be permitted to act alone, without orders."

Thirty minutes then forty-five minutes went by.

"What could he be doing?" the prosecutor asked of no one in particular.

The rain had stopped and the sun was shining. I checked the geckos on the wall, but they too had grown tired of waiting and had left.

I said to our interpreter, Kiempo, "Please go find him for us. Ask if he will be much longer."

Kiempo left the room and when he returned he was shaking his head and smiling. "Mr. Ron, you should come with me."

"What is it?"

"I cannot explain, you must come and see."

We followed Kiempo down the dark staircase to the main floor and then outside. He led us to the back of the building, where the ground was higher and therefore had not turned into pools of water in the deluge. A volleyball net was strung over the mud in the back and four men were playing, sliding and sometimes falling on the slippery surface. To avoid muddying their pants or sarongs, they had each taken off their lower garment and were left wearing what appeared to be boxer shorts. One of the players was our judge.

"What in God's name?" I said aloud.

The special prosecutor burst out laughing. "He is playing volleyball," he said. "In his underwear."

"Mmmmm," Basil replied, and then let out a curt chuckle.

"Where are his pants? Why...?"

We stood transfixed as a game took place before us, the players punching and smacking with open palms at what looked like a soccer ball. They were obviously struggling to keep the game going, sliding as they were over the wet ground.

This went on for some minutes. Then I said, "Kiempo, please speak to him. We will wait in front. Ask him what is going on, why he is doing this." I suspected the answer but needed to hear the judge say it.

The three of us, now comic characters, walked to the front of the building, where a contingent of armed Indonesian rangers, undoubtedly fresh from their own atrocities in East Timor, had fanned out to protect our backs and the prisoner. Blue berets and arm patches for international legitimacy.

Kiempo finally came to us. He was again shaking his head. "He says he cannot do this. Please do not ask him."

"Why?" I asked.

"He is afraid, Mr. Ron. He cannot take this decision. It is too big for him. We should leave him."

As Basil had said, faced with an independent decision, this judge had backed down. In his world, he understood that the nature of the decision and the person before him being judged mattered less than the act of doing something independent and outside the totalitarian chain of command in which he had lived his life, and judged his cases.

Although we did subsequently find a judge to issue a temporary order, when we returned to that same judge to extend the order, he refused to take jurisdiction. He merely sat in his car outside the courthouse, waiting for us to leave. We later learned that the minister of justice had directed that the judge refrain from hearing the case and he did what he was told. Independent thinking in the judiciary would not be tolerated.

We then ended up without a lawfully sanctioned arrest. The UN was then the subject of criticism from international human rights organizations such as Human Rights Watch and Amnesty International for our arrest and illegal detention of the prisoner. The irony of our direct action in making an arrest was evident. Criticized for inactivity and complacency in human rights enforcement, when we finally took a step, we stepped in shit.

IV.
GOD, LAW, AND MAGIC

IN GOD, NOT LAW

(Dushanbe, Tajikistan—December, 1998)

I walk down the broken steps of my apartment building on my way to the street. The staircase is six flights of concrete stairs. The walls are pock-marked with the tracings of gunplay in the building. The neighbours told me, in their broken English, how fighters had been chased up the stairs and how a gun battle had raged on this staircase. The men who ran were trapped and ran out of ammunition. They tried to make it to the roof but could not. They tried to surrender and were butchered in this staircase. The neighbours pointed out the brown blotches—permanent stains.

"Who were they?" I asked.

"Fighters," was the only answer. Anyone with a gun was a fighter, and sides did not matter to the civilians who stood by in shock and watched the savagery.

The neighbours in my building are friendly enough, given that much of their time is spent behind the safety of their steel doors. But not so my neigh-bour immediately across. I have never seen her, and except for the echo of her door opening or closing, never heard her. I assumed she was a woman, mostly because of the fear I sensed through the clanging shut of her door,

139

the haste with which she shut it, the need to shut it before I was up the stairs and could see her. Each time I left my apartment, slamming shut my own prison door, I was halfway down the stairs before I heard her door slowly unlatch and open. The squeaks of the rusted metal hinges gave away her attempt at stealth. She was looking to see me, to watch me as I walked down the staircase steps. I tried looking back when I heard the familiar sounds, but each time the door seemed already closed or only opened a crack. I became curious about her, about who she was and what she looked like. I was determined to one day see and speak with her.

The stairwell is always damp and cold and I skip down the steps two at a time. I pass the cracked and pitted walls and the window with its missing pane of glass. I run my hand over the wood banister, blackened from the oil and rubbed smooth by countless hands.

On the next landing, a Tajik cleaning woman is bent double, swaying with the side-to-side movements of a rag she uses to wash the floor. Her head is covered with a brightly flowered headscarf, the same pattern as her full-length smock, dragging along the floor as she wipes. I edge around her, feeling guilty for walking on her newly cleaned floor. A raw wind blows in through the broken windowpane over the very spot she works. Once past her I touch the wall to steady my gait and a cascade of plaster falls, crumbles at my touch, and tumbles down her clean stairs. I look back to face the rebuke of the woman but her head is bent to the work of washing with the ragged piece of cloth, back and forth.

Out in the street, a strong stench of decay and rot greets me. A dumpster beside my building overflows with garbage that is never taken away. It is the base of a volcano of refuse that is growing over and around the dumpster, attracting dogs and sallow stickmen who come to pick the bounty. How do the marginalized survive in a country of such poverty? I buy *lypioska* bread from the gypsies pushing baby carriages and I hand one loaf over to one of these men. Each time I make this token gesture the man will take the bread gingerly as though a trap is set to spring on him.

I wave down a microbus and it pulls over. It is a squat, rickety microbus, a green beetle, the locals call it, and for 100 rubles I can be driven across the city. I pay the driver and take my seat amongst the ten others crammed inside. I hold on as the driver tears down Rudaki Street. The windows are open and the breeze feels cold. I relish it, the numbing of an icy wind. I need the bracing air to clear my thoughts for what lies ahead.

I am off to a meeting between academics, government officials, and United Tajik Opposition members. The subject is the adoption of a new constitution for the country, one of the preconditions to the holding of elections and a key component to the General Agreement on the Establishment of Peace and National Accord. But there has been a stumbling block that has brought out an intellectual conflict, threatening a much wider-spread breakdown in the peace process. The clash between secularism and a commitment to theocracy in the constitution has caused rancorous debate and stalemate. The Tajiks are divided on the basic principle of secularism. Fearful of a party elected into power that would impose sharia law and a theocracy, the former communists, who make up the present government, will not agree to move ahead unless secularism is acknowledged as a founding principle of Tajikistan. The Islamic Party and opposition, both proponents of a theocratic state, will not agree.

With a stalemate at the political level, we are attempting to keep discussion open in committee meetings and at grassroot sessions held with academics and other political leaders. In the past, I have been to the committees and have discussed for hours with opposition politicians the possible meanings of secularism. I have obtained a decision from the European Human Rights Court decreeing that secularism is not the same thing as atheist dictatorship. The recognition of the separation of church and government through a secular state meant no more than that the relationship between government and governed would be through the rule of law, and not deity. But the opposition members have countered with the question of where that left a political party based on religious doctrine, believing in sharia law. If the opposition Islamic Party came to power, their authority over the people would be through God, not law. The question was difficult to answer, and it was posed by the moderates in the opposition, not the religious extremists. The opposition leadership understood that, though a small minority in their coalition aspired to sharia law, the possibility of obtaining the goal of theocracy was much more important than its actual realization, which, the leaders believed, would never occur. The fighters who had turned the tide on the annihilation of the opposition were aligned to the mullahs—Islamic religious leaders—in the coalition and so had to be placated. Secularism could not be a founding principle of the country.

Our proposal to minimize the opposition's concerns about religious freedoms took the form of strengthening the language that guaranteed these freedoms and shifting the presence of the word *secularism* to the preamble in the constitution. We surmised that placing the term there would dilute its overall effect in the document. None of this was accepted. The word itself reverberated too historically for the Islamic side.

A parallel debate was taking place in the existing parliament, called Majlis-I Oli, over the Law on Political Parties. Little more than a rubber stamp for the dictatorship of President Rahmanov, parliament was considering the addition of wording to this law that would effectively neutralize the political aspirations of religious-based political parties. "Political parties and their members have no right to use religious organizations in their activities," read the amendment to the law. This would mean the virtual elimination of the main opposition political party, which had mullahs, in their fold. All our diplomatic means were being exerted to have this provision reconsidered.

Here was the great divide that foreshadowed the clash of ideologies that lay ahead in the post-September 2001 landscape. Played out in Tajikistan, as it had been played out for centuries in Central Asia, was the end game of the religious divide. For it was here that moderate Islam became aligned with communism and went to war against radical Islam. And it was here, in a country barely known to the West and a mere footnote to the effects of Russia's "near abroad" policy, that the dilemma of the coming age was being fought and decided. Radical Islam in Tajikistan had roots in war and self-preservation. It reflected a small minority of Tajiks, but had spiritually sustained the warrior caste who had fought off the Russians. These men had to be reckoned with in any compromise for peace. Rahmanov's government sought to extinguish fundamentalism's role in peace by outlawing religious-based political parties. This could never be accepted by the opposition and could lead to further conflict. After the killing that had gone on in the mountains, the fighters were not about to compromise their spiritual base.

The constitutional challenge was much the same: every word with a religious connotation was charged. We chose our language in these debates with great caution, even though our power in this process was limited to an occasional suggestion or gentle prod.

The microbus pulls over beside the Dushanbe Turkish bakery, a haven for Turkish coffee, sweets, and bread. Across from the university, the site of the conference, I disembark and make my journey across the wide boulevard. Jawid, my interpreter, is already there, waiting for me.

"It is in here," says Jawid, leading me into one of the unmarked buildings on the campus that looks to me indistinguishable from the other drab-looking unnamed buildings. I follow him into a dark corridor. When my eyes adjust I see the shadowy forms of students standing, sitting, playing cards, talking in the cold of the lightless, heatless interior. Everyone wears a coat. Some of them sit on a ledge near an open window writing, paper held on their laps. I have unbounded admiration for their drive to be educated and mention this to Jawid. He laughs and says, "What else will they do today? Don't think it so great. Anyway, university in Canada is not like this?"

I think of heated classrooms and vast libraries, and computers and endless options and working lights. "No," I say. "Students must pay to attend."

"Really?" he says, in genuine surprise.

We find the conference room. The session has been organized by Professor Haidar Rustamov, a young progressive thinker in Tajikistan and someone I will come to befriend. In the past, he has spoken openly about the intellectual and spiritual corruptions of his government and society, and aspires to run for office when elections are held. He is courageous and dynamic and I am afraid for him. It is a wonder he has remained alive under such an intolerant regime. But the fact that he has and that he remains able to be openly critical shows me the confidence of the president. It also shows me that Rustamov really poses no threat. He is safe because he achieves little progress in his attempts at undermining the president's absolute power.

The tables are pushed close together and thirty or more of us sit huddled for warmth, and the discussions begin. Jawid sits at my ear whispering his translations of what is said. The discussion is sophisticated and intense and focuses on aspects of constitutional reform, including due process rights, of which Tajikistan has none. I speak on the topic of habeas corpus and the power of judges to review grounds of detention immediately and without

excuse. The law must be resolute and the presumption of innocence absolute, I say. At similar sessions around the world, United Nations' lawyers
are preaching the same gospel of rights, formalized in the International Cov-
enant of Civil and Political Rights. The words sound hollow to say them,
and even meaningless here. The prosecutor, also a speaker at the conference,
points that out to me when he attacks.

"How can the police do their job and protect the public," he cajoles, "if
we cannot hold a prisoner for investigation? They must have time to gather
evidence."

The room waits for the question to be translated. There is a tension now,
I can feel it before Jawid delivers the words.

"Yes. Of course," I answer. "But they must also have some reason for
wanting to arrest the man. They can only take away liberty with reason,
and it is for a judge to assess that reason. It is a way of keeping the police
honest."

Jawid stumbles over some of the words I have chosen and I am unsure
how much of what I say is passed along. The answer comes back.

"Honest? You propose a system that doubts the police over a criminal.
That makes no sense." He folds his arms at me. The room feels much hotter
now. "We live in a mountainous country. A criminal need only flee the city
for the mountains and the case is lost. The police have to act quickly, that
is all."

"I do not disagree. But a judge must sanction their action."

"Your idea helps criminals escape. Is that how Western countries
function?"

A hand bends upwards from a grey-haired man who has been sitting,
watching me closely throughout the exchange with the prosecutor. He is recognized by the chair and begins to speak. Jawid leans over and says, "Oh.
He is a judge. This will be interesting."

As Mr. Justice Aslonov of the Dushanbe municipal court speaks, the prosecutor flushes and Professor Rustamov smiles. The judge's words come to
me through Jawid; he says, "The constitutional reform you suggest is good
and I support it. The police cannot be trusted in Tajikistan to do right."

The Tajik people are living in a dictatorship in which the police and military can act with impunity and this judge can be killed without fear of rebuke

of any kind. He is speaking in front of a prosecutor from a Stalinesque regime. He is either very courageous or this is a show, for my benefit.

"The difficulty I have as a judge is in having my orders enforced," he continues. "Now, when I order a person released after a trial, the prison and police ignore me and do what they like. That is my biggest problem, and no changing of our constitution will affect this. This is rudimentary and structural."

I can scarcely believe what I am hearing. The line we are perpetually fed in dictatorships is that the judges are independent, the courts effective, but because of resource issues, problems occur. Give us money, the state asserts, and we can make it work. All of which is untrue, of course, except the need for money. A dictatorship cannot permit independent judges to oversee the rule of law. A dictatorship relies on the president's agents acting unhindered at every level of a system. Once any one of the judges becomes answerable to an authority beyond whims of power, the system becomes unstable. A freethinking judge can interfere with a president's whim and so is perceived as a threat. He needs to be removed.

SOCIETY OF SPIES

(Dushanbe, Tajikistan—December, 1998)

After the discussions on constitutional reform and judicial independence and secularism at the university in Dushanbe, Professor Rustamov and I discuss the judge's apparent heroism.

"It is play," answers the professor. "The judge offers no possible difficulty for them. Those the KGB want are simply arrested. Not officially and certainly not for a judge to know. I have seen him before. This judge always speaks this way." For me, mention of the KGB conjures up images of black trench coats and Maxwell Smart versus KAOS. Growing up through the Cold War with cartoon images of enemies, I found those enemies hardly believable. The fact that nuclear war between Russia and America never took place made a generation of skeptics of us. Was the threat ever truly there, or was it a conspiracy of economic oligopolies needing war to sell jet fighters? I had hardly believed the KGB even existed. But exist they did, and generations of Tajiks had felt their daily presence.

Several days after our session at the university, I see and hear first-hand the effects of the KGB on a culture on a day when the Tajik Opera gives a rare performance. The singers come out in white costumes and slowly raise bone-white china plates to the sides of their faces as they sing. The sound seems to echo from the plates and, as Jawid whispers to me, the unwashed pilaf grease from last night's dinner. The sight of those plates being raised in unison was a marvel—a piece of unity of purpose that I had not yet seen in the country. Jawid and I begin to giggle at the sight of those plates, and his joke. One of those spectacles of incongruity that sets you off, like priests lying prostrate at the front of the altar at Holy Thursday mass—sending the altar boys into peals of hysterics.

The beauty of that opera, of what people can achieve despite the horrors of what they have lived through and were living through, give those in the audience I spoke with afterwards, optimism and hope. If you can sing an aria, they reasoned, the society has not lost its desire to thrive. They were right to think that way, but I was so preoccupied at that time with getting beneath the lies we were told that I scarcely saw the beauty. The elaborate handshake greetings from our guards at the front gate; the judge's courage; the singers' range. In imagery that ought to have engendered feelings of hope, I saw only poverty of virtue. The guards mocked us with their ritual, though most of our staff did not see it; the judge was forthright and honest, but to no effect or risk; inside, the singers hit the notes, but outside, outside, heads were being cut off and left at the tank monument and a brutal dictatorship held power. What could we trust?

After the opera, Jawid and I, made hungry by his joke of pilaf grease, have an early dinner of pilaf, which is rice heavily soaked in oil and cooked in oil and served with oil and shards of lamb, themselves cooked in oil. With so much oil in me after dinner, I feel slippery and heavy with an urge to sleep.

We make our way down Chekhova Street to Rudaki, the only street we feel reasonably safe on. It is a crisp, clear winter day. The onset of winter has been easy in Dushanbe, but I have never felt so cold. A cold that seeps slowly into my skin and burrows deep to the bone. The Soviet-built apartments we live in are designed to be large and grand, with double balconies and expansive rooms and banks of windows. But the Soviet-built apartments had Soviet-supplied gas to run Soviet-maintained heating. The Soviets are gone, taking their heat with them. My apartment rarely has heat. As the fall months progress and winter comes on, the cold inches into the brickwork of the building. Nothing is there to resist it; once the double layer of bricks is penetrated by the chill, the inner walls of the rooms succumb. The concrete floors under the wood slats take the longest to freeze, but they too are conquered. Surrounded by the cold weather front within my apartment, I try to resist with layers of clothes and a cocoon sleeping bag that keeps me wrapped tight as a bug all night. But I remain cold. My heels are perpetually freezing knobs of flesh.

Rudaki Street is a wide tree-lined boulevard that crests at the centre of the city and reaches out at either end to white-capped mountains. Riding the crest are houses of power—the presidential palace, an enormous white-and-gold structure gleaming in the afternoon sun, like the smile of a rich, fat, gold-toothed merchant in a poor country. Further along is Majlis-I Oli—parliament. It is in here during a critical vote on the election law that I will witness the bluntness of tyranny. There is no subtlety when tyranny reigns, only size and belligerence matter. The president will shout down his opponents and they will submit, but as they leave parliament, their red faces steam with hatred.

As Jawid and I meander our way back to the UN bunker, Jawid stops to speak with someone who seems to be a friend. They shake hands and embrace, as is the Tajik custom between men. I stand discreetly to one side and watch the Ladas careening past us on the street. At this time of day the street is crowded with electric buses and cars, windows blackened.

The cars are black demons. They veer in and out, dodging pedestrians who seem oblivious to the perils on this road. It is as if vehicles appeared overnight in Dushanbe and caught everyone by surprise. The people step off the curb without looking and simply meander into the road as if crossing an empty mountain trail. It reveals the nomad in them—the Tajik people are simple wanderers.

Jawid says goodbye to his friend. They shake hands and embrace once again. As the friend walks away, Jawid appears uncomfortable. He is blushing slightly and will not look at me.

Finally, I say to Jawid, "What is it?"

He answers immediately. "That man was my friend in university, two years ago. I have not seen him since." Jawid looks at me as though this information should explain everything.

"Yes. Good," I say. "But ... why do you seem uncomfortable?"

Jawid laughs, "Because I lied to him. He asked me what I was doing. He meant for work. It is the usual and only question we Tajiks ask each other. These days."

Jawid's habit of stopping mid-idea in the expectation that I can easily fill in the blanks continuously frustrates me. I prod him. "You lied ... about what?"

Jawid smiles and says, "My job. I told him I was not working."

"Why?" I ask.

"I ... don't know. It is the usual answer. He said the same for himself.... I do not believe him. He probably does not believe me." Seeing my confusion, he adds, "It is normal in this country to answer this way."

Still, I am not getting it. "But why?" I ask. "Is it because of the UN work? Are you concerned that people know?" The relatively luxurious life of a UN worker amidst the poor of Tajikistan irritated some.

"Not that. Of course not," he says quickly. "It is just ... our way. You see, Ron, why should he know what I am doing? It is not his business. I cannot know what he does with this information. It is better to be guarded."

"Because you may be robbed?"

Jawid shakes his head. "No, not money. Although yes, sure, why not? Perhaps that is one reason. The rest, who knows?" He gives me a big shrug. "In the past, under Russia, it was always better to reveal nothing. Any information can be used, somehow, in some way. It remains the same now. To be safe, we lie about everything. One never knows who will report you, or what they will say."

"We lie about everything."

"The only truth in newspapers is the date on the top of the front page."

The words come back to me as I listen to Jawid. A Vietnamese refugee in Chi Ma Wan refugee camp on Lantau Island was trying hard to explain life in Vietnam under a repressive system. We were in an overcrowded camp in the British colony of Hong Kong. The Vietnamese were stuffed into rounded, breadbox-shaped metal quarters that baked in the South Asian sun. Rows of triple-tiered bunk beds lined both sides of the container. Entire families slept in one, hot, cramped tier.

"It is saying in Hanoi," the refugee said to me. "The government controls the newspapers and fills it with lies. They cannot lie about the date."

"So who do you trust?" I asked him.

He smiled at me and said, "The old ladies who sell fish in the markets. You cannot lie about fish."

The lies in Tajikistan are on a different scale. They are mundane exchanges of absences of information between ordinary people. These absences act as a shield from reproach for doing or saying or believing the wrong thing. The KGB had made Tajikistan a society of spies. The spy could be your neighbour or your girlfriend or the butcher you made one brief comment to, or he could be your old college friend you happen to bump into on Rudaki Street as you return from lunch. Allegiances and power change quickly in Tajikistan. Political allegiances teeter precariously inside a Stalinesque system of informants. The only way to rise in society is to be connected. Information is the currency. Information about disloyalty is a gold bar. Better to keep your mouth shut. Better to be unemployed and unopinionated.

Jawid and I continue down the street, two easygoing fellows without jobs and with nothing to say going to find a place to snooze off the heavy effects of a pilaf lunch.

I AM NEIGHBOUR

(Dushanbe, Tajikistan—January 1999)

I am inside the safety of my steel door, waiting for my call sign. Emboldened by the courage of my nightly vodka shot, I decide not to answer, to see how fast our reaction force come bursting through my door to save my life.

"Charlie Lima One, come in, over."

At last, my moment. I wait, watching the red light on my hand-held radio flickering.

"Charlie Lima One, come in." I know that UN staff throughout Dushanbe are listening, wondering: is he dead?

On my end of the communication network, only silence.

"Charlie Papa One, come in over." The next in line after me is being called, Jozef's call sign. They have given up on me. No doubt other security officers are busily loading weapons and contacting Tajik police for a SWAT-like intervention into my apartment.

After an hour waiting for my rescuers to come, I hear a gentle tap on my door. At last, I think, someone does care!

I pull the heavy steel bolt back with a clang, draw the inside door open, and push out the outer door, expecting to see a group of well-armed and soon-to-be angry men, carrying M16s, the UN security weapon of choice. For an instant I think of telling them I had heard armed men trying to enter the apartment and so had to hide in a closet, under a bed, on the balcony and, in fearful silence, could not get to the hand-held radio.

I misplaced it.

Battery ran out.

Forgot my call sign.

A middle-aged, very short woman stands on the other side of the doorway. "Sorry to disturb," she says. "I am neighbour." She half turns to the open door across the hall.

My sense of relief at the sight of her washes over me and I smile broadly. "Hello!" I say, too cheerfully.

It takes a moment, but I soon realize who I am speaking with. It is the mysterious woman who opens her door each time I leave my apartment and who has been watching me since I arrived in this building. I can see through to her open doorway and into a lit hallway and to the back of her apartment. No one stands in the doorway or in the room. She seems to be alone.

"My English is bad," she says. "Forgive me."

"No. No. Please. Do you want to come in?" I am so pleased not to be lying to our security officers.

"Yes. Thank you."

I step aside to allow her in. "Your door?" I say gesturing to her open door.

She waves at it. "Downstairs door is now lock. Very safe."

We sit in my kitchen and I make her tea. "Sorry to disturb," she says again. "I have seen you. You work for UN. *Da?*"

"*Da.*" One of my two Russian words.

"My life is very terrible," she says without emotion. "My husband is died and I have no family left here. I am Russian. But live in Tajikistan all my life. No one in Russia. I want leave Tajikistan. Can you help?"

"To get to Russia?"

"I am very afraid here," she says, ignoring me. "I am Russian. I could be killed. Killed for this apartment even. I am very scared."

"Do you have anyone in Russia?"

"No. I no like communism. I want go to America. Can you help? I will be safe in America."

"I am not American," I say.

"Oh, then what?"

"Canada."

"Canada? Oh, yes, sure I know. Canada. But you are UN people. Can you help me?"

I explain to her the legal process of being accepted as a refugee in the West. A protection officer from the United Nations High Commissioner for Refugees in Tajikistan would interview her and decide whether or not she meets the UN definition of a refugee. He would want to know whether she has a well-founded fear of persecution by reason of her political opinion, membership in a social group, nationality, religious or ethnic group. Being afraid isn't enough to garner international protection. Everyone in Tajikistan is afraid.

Listening intently to my explanation, my neighbour sips at her tea, thinks carefully and then says, "Can you help me?"

"I can introduce you to the UNHCR protection officer in Dushanbe. She will interview you and decide if she can help." My neighbour wrinkles her face at me. She is hearing a bureaucrat pass her off to another bureaucrat, a feature of daily life in the communist Soviet Union, Central Asia, Tajikistan. To her ears, I have signalled that nothing will be done. As I say the words, I know that this is how it must sound to her. And as I say the words, I also know that UNHCR would do nothing for her. Recognizing that a person is a genuine refugee inside a country like Tajikistan means casting blame on the government for either being a party to persecution or being ineffective in its ability to protect its own citizens. Such international chastisement would rarely take place while the UNHCR remained in a country. Embarrassed by the allegation, as hopefully they would be, the dictatorship that ran this country would defend itself, condemn the UNHCR and then make life miserable for the organization. Visas cancelled by a stroke. Supplies lost at the airport. Protection officer expelled. It would take the strongest of refugee cases for UNHCR to act for my neighbour, and being a Russian afraid for her future in Tajikistan would not be enough.

She senses my hesitation.

"I will talk to UNHCR tomorrow, if you like. Ask them to speak with you."

She begins to nod. "*Da*. Thank you, sir. Sorry to disturb." She stands to go.

"I will talk to them tomorrow, I promise," I say quickly, desperately wanting to disabuse her of my own worst fear, that I have become my worst fear, a UN bureaucrat. I think that if I speak quickly enough and convincingly enough, I will cast off the insidious cloak of the bureaucrat and be a human being.

She is walking out my door. "*Da*. Thank you. I wait for you." She enters her apartment and her door clangs shut. The hallway echoes with the sound. I make an oath to myself while the echo still sounds that I will pursue her case with UNHCR, make all the contacts for her, convince them to take her case seriously.

But I know they won't.

I close my own door as softly as I can, not wanting to disturb anyone in the building with the reverberations of a steel door banging shut at this late hour. I want to be unobtrusive and co-operative and helpful to my neighbours. I want to feel that I am somehow helping someone with something. I then return to my darkness and my thoughts and waiting for UN security to show up at my door to make sure I am safe.

But by now, I know they won't.

MONKEY SOLDIERS

(Dushanbe, Tajikistan—1998)
(Phnom Penh, Cambodia—1991)

When I returned to Canada from Cambodia in 1994 I was visited nightly by ghostly apparitions—two women in large-brimmed hats coming to me with heads bowed in profound sadness. Each time they arrived I would get out of bed to make sure they weren't real and as I approached they would invariably fade and disappear. After several months, I finally stopped seeing them. Here in Dushanbe, five years later, they return to me.

It is 4 a.m. when I awake to these visions in my room. They wear the same large-brimmed hats they had on in Montreal, and they have the same angled bodies and position of close proximity to one another. I have to go to them, to make sure they are not real, and so I brave leaving the warm, tight wrapping of blankets I have piled around me and endure the sharp pain of a cold floor. As I approach, they leave, as they always have done, dissolving into the dark. Jesus, I think, my head spinning from vodka reflux, a frozen floor and my mind's endless doubts. How can they be appearing again? I had relied on science and decided, years earlier, after their first visitation in Montreal, that they were quirks of shadows played upon a wall by the dull glow of a streetlight outside my window on Prince Arthur Street. But now they are here in Dushanbe, and they are the same as they had been: the same hats, downcast heads, sorrow. I let the implications float past. I will not believe in ghosts.

I investigated so many murders in Cambodia and saw so much death while I was there. One young boy we had found tied to a tree in the province of Ratanikiri, shot dead. At first we thought that the killing was motivated by politics but we came to learn that he was killed because a motorcycle-smuggling operation had gone bad along the Vietnamese-Cambodian border. The boy had had his motorcycle stolen and then his own shirt was used to tie him to a tree before he was shot.

The Vietnamese army, so confident and impenetrable, had met with us on their side of the border and, over early morning whisky shots from large glass bottles in which dead cobras were curled, told us they knew that a smuggling ring was operating, that motorbikes were being stolen right from under their riders, and how the riders ended up dead. They would catch them, the Vietnamese captain assured me, and cut their throats. I had little doubt.

We went to see the mother of the dead boy. Her husband was in the political opposition, so we needed to make sure this was not a political attack. The boy's mother was ironing a shirt when we came in, with the kind of iron that is heated by coals stuffed in the back. No electricity. She kept saying that she had ironed her son's shirt the day he died and that they had used that shirt to tie him up. She kept pressing hard on the garment she was ironing, tears rolling down her cheeks.

In Asia I came to understand the concepts of spirits and hauntings in a new light, and to take them very seriously. I felt and witnessed their effects.

Our Thai secretarial staff at the UN in Bangkok were ardent Buddhists and deeply spiritual. Cambodia terrified them because, they believed, unhappy spirits roamed its interiors. Too many unburied dead. Too many murdered souls. Too much blood. Spirit houses lay broken and discarded by the Khmer Rouge and temples looted. The dead were angry.

When we flew into Phnom Penh in September 1991, our Thai secretary Joom was crying. We checked into the Hotel Cambodiana and as I closed the door to her room on our first day in country she was sitting on the bed looking out a window and rocking back and forth. "Joom," I called to her. "I will come by later, after you're settled." Joom was a mature, middle-aged woman with decades of time in the UN. She was highly organized, efficient and tough. Joom would keep us productive in a land where phones worked for twenty minutes and electricity faded to black most of the day. In the months prior to a massive influx of UN peacekeepers into the country, we were here to save face and report on the humanitarian needs of the country after decades of international isolation and embargo.

The Thais have an awkward relationship with their Khmer neighbours. The way they see their relationship is this: they live beside a dysfunctional family whose son became a mass murderer. Although overall they are richer and more secure than their Cambodian cousins, they fear what lurks within Cambodia. At least the Bangkok dwellers I met felt that way. When the rollicking, invincible Vietnamese army appeared at the Thai border in their hunt for Pol Pot in 1979, the Thais panicked. Under hypnotic control of a puppet royal family manipulated by army general puppeteers, the Thai populace believed the Vietnamese to be evil people who ate their young and defiled the spirits. A large part of the US-Vietnam war was fought from US bases in Thailand. The Thai military elite grew rich from those bases and needed support for their own war against communist insurgents. So throughout Thailand, anti-Vietnamese propaganda was spread with thick dollops of lies and half-truths. A domino theory was born: Thailand would fall to the armies of Ho Chi Minh as vanguard for Mao's conquest of Asia.

Joom grew to maturity under the shadow of the dominoes. As a girl, she prayed and made offerings for protection against the Vietnamese and their demon spirits. She had listened to reports of the killing fields of Cambodia and she had burned more incense. With the Vietnamese at the Thai border, she went to temple every day. Now, cruelly, we had brought her into the country of her darkest dreams.

When I returned to her hotel later that night, nothing I had seen so far prepared me for what awaited inside.

The doorman, a young Khmer who had earlier seen me bring Joom to the hotel, opened the door for me, allowing the first billows of air-conditioned spirits to come frolicking out. He smiled and touched my arm, an act highly uncharacteristic for the Khmer. "She is scared here, sir," he said.

"What?" I said.

"She scared. Your wife. She left hotel one hour ago. She walk around the grounds. She walk to fence." He pointed to the perimeter. "Then come back. Cry. Very much."

"Not my wife," I said.

He shrugged.

"What happened?" I asked.

He shrugged again.

"Where is she now?"

"Went up elevator," he said. "Not stop cry."

"Thank you," I said.

"Goodbye," he said, smiling.

I turned and walked through the sterile lobby of the Cambodiana to the bank of elevators. The hotel bore no resemblance to the city and country outside. Shiny marbled floor. Baskets of fruit. Tailored doormen. After being solicited for "ic'ream" in the mud of the back streets of the city, I understood the incongruity of the hotel scene now more than ever. It was clean. It was safe. And it had lights. The dark city of Phnom Penh lurked beyond the torchlit gates.

At the door to her room I knocked. "Joom," I called softly. "It's me, Ron."

I knocked again. "Joom," I said more loudly this time. "Are you in there?"

I heard a shuffling from the room, then silence. "Lon?" she called out. "Lon?"

"Yes, Joom, " I said. "Open the door."

I listened to the lock being turned and the muted wump, wump, wump of feet running on carpet. The door remained closed.

"Joom?" I tried the handle and it gave. Slowly pushing it forward, I stepped through and into her room. Joom was nowhere to be seen.

"Jesus," I whispered, conjuring up my own deity as I surveyed the field of what looked like a great battle. The room was small with a wall-sized window facing the city. The curtains had been pulled completely to one side. Typically in these rooms two single beds had been set up side by side, separated by a night table. But in Joom's room one bed had been turned on its side and leaned against the wall. The other had a large mound in its centre where bed clothing had been piled high. The night table was lying face down between the beds. On the floor lay scattered every moveable item in the room: the phone, ashtray, cushions, lamp, and the sundries of a hotel. A small fridge stood by one wall, its door ajar. On top lay the discarded remains of empty beer cans. What is this? I thought. I had never known Joom to touch alcohol.

Expecting to find her there, I walked to the window and looked behind the curtains, then pulled them closed.

The only other place she could be was under the mound on the second bed.

"Joom," I called softly, pulling gingerly at the coverings. She moved and pulled against me in a tug-of-war for the blankets.

"Joom, what is it?"

A muffled response came from under the protective mound.

Not wishing to push her further, I pulled down the adjacent bed and sat. "I'm here, Joom," I said. "Nothing to be afraid of."

But there was.

Peoples identify themselves by significant events in their histories. The easy ones to note from outside are wars, the birth of nationhood, the death of leaders. The harder ones are less tangible. Not events, but representations. Great speeches, poems, epic stories, myths, and miracles. Asia has its epic odyssey, the *Ramakien*. It is the story of two kingdoms, one inhabited by men and the other by demons. The kingdoms are themselves in perpetual conflict over control and destiny of the world. The evil demons are led by a giant called Tosakan and fight the forces of good, who are monkey soldiers under allegiance to a Monkey King. In the end, evil is vanquished and the Monkey King victorious, but not before evil wins its share of battles. Demons can be beaten, the Thais learned, but not before coming into your room once in a while.

I found myself sitting in the middle of a Ramakien that Joom had evoked into being in her hotel room. Monkey soldiers were fighting demons in her room, she would finally confide in me. But the demons were winning and coming for her, through the glass of the windows, the TV set, the walls. But not just them. The unclean spirits of the many murdered in Cambodia were also here. They were unhappy as they had not been properly buried. They were hungry as there was little if any food left in spirit houses in this poor country. They were tortured; they had been murdered in gruesome ways. Joom saw and heard them inside her room that night. They were hissing at her, she told me.

Of course, the beer didn't help. In fact, when she did emerge from under the blankets I saw immediately that she was drunk.

"Joom," I said with a smile. "You're drunk. I can't believe it." And I couldn't.

It was as if your proper maiden aunt, whose morality squeezed through her frowns at you, had come to Christmas dinner drunk and knocked over the tree. I had never seen Joom drink or let her guard down.

"Khun Lonny...," she pleaded with me. "Don't leave me, *na*? Don't leave. They are here. They are everywhere. Please." Then, looking to the curtain I had closed, she shrieked and ran towards it. "The demons must be able to leave," she cried. "Let them out...!"

After opening the curtains she raced back to her bed and curled into a ball. I could see that she was shaking.

"Joom, don't worry, I'll stay," I told her. "I'll sleep right here." But the last thing I wanted was to be in that room.

"Yes good. Good. Please, Khun Lon. Please."

I sank back into the bed and tried to think of what to do. She was too drunk and unpredictable to try to get her out of the room. Would it even make a difference? Probably not; the monkey soldiers were everywhere.

My bed sagged and I felt Joom sliding in next to me. "Please," she said, putting her arm around me. "I am too scare...."

I jumped up and out of bed. "Look. There are no spirits here. I am sure of it. And ... ah, I can't stay...." I had to get out of there. "You're drunk, Joom. Go to sleep."

"Nooooo ..." she called to me as I headed out the door, closing it behind me with a thump, like the sound of a great monkey king pounding its chest.

V.
THE TRIAL IN TAJIKISTAN

THEY HAVE CONFESSED

(Dushanbe, Tajikistan—February, 1999)

"My son is innocent," the old man says to me, *chapan* coat wrapped tight against the winter wind. "He is a good boy. He could not kill UN people."

I am standing outside of Dushanbe Central Prison, Sizo No. 1, on the morning of February 25, 1999. The trial of three men accused of killing Team Garm begins this morning inside the prison walls. The three are soldiers of the opposition army. They were arrested on September 1, 1998, six weeks after the killing. They are from the mountainous regions of central Tajikistan—opposition territory. They were told by their United Opposition Field Commander, Mullo Abdullo, to go into Dushanbe and hand themselves over to government police. They were told that they would be asked a few questions about their role in the July 20 ambush and killing of UN personnel in Tavildara.

It is now almost six months later and they remain in detention and on trial for their lives. We have heard reports that they have been severely tortured while in detention, yet the opposition leadership has been oddly silent. No complaints to the government about their treatment. No accusations of deceit. In a political climate in which accusations fly between the two sides over the slightest misstep, there is not a word from the men who sent the three boys to Dushanbe and into the custody of the government.

I have repeatedly asked to see these men, to confirm or refute the reports of torture. My requests have been denied.

Prior to the trial, in early January, 1999, I view a videotape of the confession of one of the men. It is proudly played for me by the prosecutor (called procurator) on the case to allay my concerns that the confessions were coerced. We watch the video in his large blue office on the fourth floor of the ministry of justice. To reach the prosecutor's floor, Jawid and I climb a dark and broken staircase at the back of the building. We enter a vestibule to his office where a woman sits pecking at a large, ancient typewriter. Along one wall two men in leather coats lounge on a purple couch. They are both clutching manila folders and watching a small black-and-white TV in the corner of the room.

Jawid announces us to the woman and we sit to watch TV. A Russian game show is playing. Contestants line two sides of a railway track leading to a cage the size of a jail cell. Inside the cage the game's moderator is perched on a high stool. Occasionally he leaves the stool to climb onto the bars and hang, simian-like, as he asks the questions, none of which I can understand. The contestants, about twenty in total, stand in two rows facing each other. Between them runs the track. At the front of the lines a dwarf stands, dressed in a tuxedo. Each time a contestant is chosen to answer a question, the dwarf brings him forward beyond a velvet rope barrier and then escorts him back again to his place in the line.

The winner of the game receives a pile of gold bars on a railway car.

The game begins with a large lizard making its way down the track. By some act of magic the lizard turns into the dwarf and the game starts.

The phone rings and the woman stops typing to answer.

"*Da,*" she says and the two on the couch are told to go in. They take one last look at the game show before disappearing through a silver-studded, red-leather-padded door.

Our turn with the prosecutor comes before a winner emerges from beside the railway track. Jawid is disappointed to miss the conclusion of the game and he blushes as we pass through the studded door. On the other side a small man dressed in a suit that is much too large for him greets us. He has carefully chosen to remain behind his desk for our entry and then to move in front for a greeting. We do little more than shake hands before one of his three phones rings. It is a phone from the same era as the typewriter in his waiting room, a large rotary-dial, emerald-green hunk of plastic that looks more like a movie prop than a working means of communication. Its ring is loud and hollow-sounding and comes in bursts of three. A row of plastic buttons sits at the base of the phone requiring a hard push at the one that flashes. He struggles with the button until it snaps down and connects him. He then raises the oversized handset to his ear, and in so doing conceals a good portion of the side of his head.

A file lies open on his desk and as the prosecutor talks on the phone, I survey the upside-down images. The open page contains a drawing of a vehicle, the letters UN written on the side, and the outline of one body on what appears to be a road. The vehicle sits in the middle of the road. On the side of the road men are kneeling and pointing weapons. Emerging from these weapons, lines are drawn converging at the vehicle and the body. The sketch depicts what I guess to be the prosecution's theory of the murder. In this brief glimpse, I obtain more information of what the prosecution thinks happened than we have received in six months. The government has been extremely reluctant to reveal to us the substance of its investigations, prompting some within the UN to speculate on government complicity in the killing. I have my doubts that that is the reason for their reticence. Their entire system of justice is built upon secrecy and deceit. It is a reflex the bureaucrats running the system cannot easily discard. For now I am willing to assume that is all it is.

From my understanding of this drawing, the prosecution theory seems to be that three of the four UN members were shot inside the vehicle while the fourth was killed outside. Why was the fourth outside, I wonder, and how do they know? The bodies were found away from the vehicle in the ravine below. Did that mean that they were taken out of the vehicle after being shot and thrown down the cliffside? Or did they tumble out when their vehicle rolled down the hillside? Among UN personnel, speculations about the killing abound. One such speculation is that the body of at least one of the deceased had markings consistent with torture and strangulation. Perhaps the killers took the men out alive and tortured them before finishing them off. But why?

The prosecutor sees my interest in the file and casually closes it. His conversation ended, he replaces the handset and it instantly rings again.

"We are very busy catching criminals," he says to me in Russian. Jawid translates.

When our discussion finally begins, the prosecutor commences with a stream of well-aimed rhetoric. He starts by accusing the UN of not providing him with evidence gathered by our police arriving at the crime scene in Tavildara. He lectures me about the need for co-operation and how the job they are attempting earnestly to carry out has been made more difficult and maybe impossible because of UN actions. The UN, he tells me, would not permit an autopsy of the bodies. His hands are tied, he says, until he receives our full co-operation.

The communist systems I have encountered seem to precipitate rhetoric. In 1989 I sat in Hanoi before officials of the Ministry of Education of the Republic of Vietnam. As part of a delegation from the United Nations High Commissioner for Refugees I was in Hanoi with the second planeload of Vietnamese refugees returning voluntarily from Hong Kong. We had enticed them with money and offers of resettlement aid to leave the confines of their razor-wire compounds, through which they could see but never touch the Marlborough man riding high on the side of Hong Kong office towers. I wanted to talk about admission criteria for secondary school and university. The Vietnamese officials began each discussion we had with reference to American B-52s and the destruction of their infrastructure by carpet bombing two decades before.

"The case is clear," the Tajik prosecutor says finally. "I have no doubt but that these men are the killers."

"How can you be sure?" I ask.

"They have confessed!" he says triumphantly. "And now, I will show you the confessions so you will know that they are true."

He turns on a TV and VCR in his office and inserts a tape. Static fills the screen and then the picture appears. A man is sitting on a slight wooden chair, his face directed at the camera. He has shoulder-length black hair and an equally long and bushy jet-black beard. It takes me a few moments to see the wound clearly, but I finally do. His nose has been freshly broken. It is red and arched in the middle and he has two black eyes.

Head bent slightly, he speaks in a quiet tone. Jawid listens and translates for me.

"I understand that I can have a lawyer," the bearded man is saying, "But I choose not to have one."

He then relates his part in the murder of four UN members on the road from Garm to Tavildara on July 20, 1998. He says they were ordered by their commander to kill them and so they did. They waited in ambush on the road and when the vehicle appeared they stopped it, shot the occupants, and pushed the vehicle over the cliff. They stole their radios and satellite communication equipment. He does not know why he received the order to kill them. He is a soldier and carries out orders, he says.

The confession lasts only a few minutes. When the tape ends the prosecutor quickly retrieves it and places it in a safe in the wall.

"Satisfied?" he asks.

"His nose," I say. "Someone broke his nose."

He looks at me and blinks. "His nose is not broken," he finally says.

"But we saw it," I say. "The tape was clear."

"No," he says, "You saw shadows, maybe. But no broken nose."

I look to Jawid, but his expression remains impassive. The prosecutor has not even attempted to offer some clever explanation. He has merely denied a fact which was undeniable. The men who interrogated the bearded man on the TV screen and had elicited his confession had broken his nose in the process—perhaps more. I am surprised, not by the evidence of torture, but by the prosecutor's indifference to the quality of his denial. It should not surprise me, however, as I have seen this type of strategy used before. To boldly deny the existence of a fact, or assert one which does not exist, pits one observer's word against another's. The fewer the number of observers, the easier it is to deny the fact. I am the first and possibly last outsider to see the tape. My complaints about what I saw will be denied. The men were not tortured, we will be told, they freely confessed. This will be repeated often enough so that eventually even the UN hierarchy may doubt what I have seen.

The Khmer Rouge in Cambodia used this tactic often. Repeat a lie often enough and it becomes truth. In their radio broadcasts they consistently and untruthfully claimed that the Vietnamese in Cambodia were soldiers planted by the Vietnamese government. Eventually Cambodians who had

lived peacefully next door to their ethnic Vietnamese neighbours for generations began suspecting them. Suspicion led to fear and finally hatred. Hatred
led to killing.

It is now February 1999, one month after my viewing of the confession in
the prosecutor's office, and the trial is set to start. The old man who approached me is the father of the boy with the broken nose, Jawid discovers.
Hands locked behind his back, he peers at me through tear-filled eyes. He
wants me to agree, to say that I can help him free his son. He has come to
Dushanbe from the mountains to convince anyone who will listen that a
mistake has been made. The opposition leadership in Dushanbe will not see
him. He has no access to the government side. So he has come to the jail, to
be at the trial, to make his case here, to me.

I look into this deeply weathered face, at the creases the mountain wind
has burned into every inch of his skin, and feel only pity.

"I can do nothing for your son," I say to him. "I am here to ensure that
the trial is fair. That's all. I have no power."

He nods, shakes my hand and smiles. "Thank you," he says, then returns
to a group of his people huddled like a frightened herd across the road. The
older men of the herd are tall and slightly stooped. They are also bearded
with crinkly white strands that fall to their waists. Some clutch at prayer
beads, twirling the well-worn wooden spheres in time to silent verses. They
wear the *tupi* skullcaps and clutch at ankle-length blue or green *chapan*
coats. The young men have moustaches and wear leather jackets. A few are
smoking. The women sit, separated from the men. Each of them is dressed
the same, in long floral dresses and brightly coloured *rumoli* headscarves.
They watch quietly as the men lean towards one another and converse in
whispers so the city will not hear them.

This caravan of people has left the safety of the mountains to come to this
place, to see their sons. In their voyage to Dushanbe, they have paid countless bribes at countless roadblocks along the mountain roads and stayed
awake for long, crowded hours in the buses that brought them, so they
would not be robbed by other passengers or cheated by the driver. In Dushanbe, they no doubt have been hounded by police and criminal gangs.
They find relations, however distant, and stay with them.

Out of place in their ancient clothes and mannerisms of politeness and dignity, they exude a purity sorely missing in Dushanbe. Even the children in this city appear tougher, more jaded than these people. Though physically large and strong-looking, they appear fragile and gentle. I want them to leave and return home. I am afraid for them.

Directly across from the mountain people wait the clean-shaven lawyers for the accused and the state, dressed in suits and leather coats and clutching at bundles of papers. They too huddle together, whispering conspiracies, staring across the road at a people that have stepped out of their own history. The width of road between the two groups spans a century of time. In the middle of the road, dividing the centuries, is a platoon of soldiers. They are a precaution against the opposition's attempt to free their men through violent action, we are told. The jail has been chosen for the trial for the same reason. Three opposition fighters face the possibility of being put to death. The government is taking no chances.

The soldiers wear a uniform I have not seen before. Jozef, the Polish policeman with me for the trial, reads the insignia on their arm crest.

"They are an elite unit," Jozef tells me. "Special forces," he says, lighting a cigarette.

Under his breath, loud enough only for me to hear, Jawid whispers, "They are killers!"

A black sedan pulls up to the prison gate and stops. The soldiers immediately fan out along the road. The doors open and the court officials step out—a Supreme Court judge, two laypersons who also preside as judges, and a court reporter. I have met the supreme court judge the day before in his chambers, so I recognize him as he steps from the car. He is a hunched little man with a huge head and watery eyes. A cigarette rests perpetually between two of his yellowed fingers. He waves at me and nods for us to follow him into the prison.

We follow through an iron door and into a dark alcove the size of a small elevator. Jawid, Jozef, and I huddle together with the judges and lawyers in the cold space waiting for the prison guards to open an inner door to the prison. The guards have not been told we are coming or that a trial is taking place in the prison. They refuse to allow us in. The supreme court judge, who in this light and in this space reminds me of a hobbit, is furious. Face turning purple, he stoops to the level of the small slit in the wall through which the conversation is taking place and shoves in his identity card.

A slit in the wall, as inconveniently placed as possible, seems to be a typical way for security to be conducted in Tajikistan. In order to enter the presidential palace to meet a member of the government, you must enter a small chamber, no more than three-foot square, and pass a piece of paper with the name of the person you are coming to visit, along with your ID card, through a narrow opening located at a height of no more than four feet off the ground. Immediately under the opening is a wide table. To reach the opening with the paper and ID card you must bend down and stretch across this table to carefully deposit the documents with your outstretched finger-tips. It requires balance and co-ordination to complete this feat without crashing down onto the table.

The guards examine the judge's ID card and shove it back through the slit so that it lands on the floor. Jawid lets out a quick laugh and turns his head to the wall. The hobbit judge stamps his foot and raises his voice, but it is no use. The prosecutor tells us to wait outside until they sort out the misunderstanding.

It is the first day of the trial.

THE QUEEN OF LAWYERS
(Dushanbe, Tajikistan—March, 1999)

Day two of the trial.

A commanding officer meets us at the front gate of the prison. He is flanked by other officers and guards with wooden batons the size of baseball bats. Our initial arrival for the first day of the trial had caught prison officials on duty that morning by surprise. There will be no mistake this time.

The inner courtyard of the prison is ringed by red brick walls that are cracked and crumbling. Razor wire is everywhere—along the inside of the walls, on top, beside a flower-lined path we are to follow. Groups of women prisoners in blue uniforms and headscarves carry bags onto a lorry. Some are smiling. The young blushing faces of the guards fix on us. We are out of place here and the young guards search for officers to reassure them.

In the guard towers there are no guards and at ground level I see no guns. The baseball bats must work well. The steel door we have just walked through clangs shut. A few of the women prisoners reflexively look to the familiar sound, then quickly turn away. Off to one side, standing alone, satchel under one arm, is a woman I have seen before. She is tall and has shoulder-length black hair. She is watching me with her black eyes. I smile and wave to her. Only her eyebrow flinches, then arches in a high crest, and a barely perceptible nod is cast my way.

She turns and moves toward the group of women. I watch her gesturing to a guard who responds by pulling on the sleeve of one of the group—pulling her to the woman. She is here to see a client, I suppose, and has found her.

I had met this lawyer one month before, in my office in Dushanbe, in my hunt for a criminal defence lawyer to represent the UN at the trial. She had not come for the job but as escort for Golbahar, the queen of lawyers in Tajikistan.

The Tajik criminal code allowed the victim and family to have representation at the criminal trial of an accused to question witnesses, introduce evidence, and make arguments. The UN had been victimized by the killing of its staff members so was permitted into the trial. I had been assigned the task of finding a Tajik lawyer to represent us.

Golbahar entered my metal cubicle that lay outside the main UN building. She was a large woman with frizzled hair that stuck up in mad sprouts. Her head was huge and at first I thought she was a man. Perhaps she was. She had stabs of bright red lipstick on her lips and circles of skin-coloured cream on her nose and cheeks. She sat with an enormous sigh in the seat across from me and immediately put a handkerchief to her mouth and dabbed. Each time she spoke, she spoke through the handkerchief. She coughed hard into the cloth several times during our meeting. She spoke in the gravelly voice of tuberculosis.

Golbahar smiled often through the cloth, and laughed at everything. She asked me where I was from. Canada, I said. This engulfed her in a sound belly laugh. Did I speak French? No. She laughed so hard she began gnawing on the handkerchief to keep some control. How old was I? Thirty-eight. She slapped her knee.

She asked me what I thought of the Clinton and the Lewinsky affair. She told me a man had to be a man and that it all seemed too silly. She snapped her fingers whenever she really enjoyed what she had just said.

The young woman with her, with black eyes, translated and helped her walk. She was studying under Golbahar. When the young woman spoke, she spoke with long slender fingers lightly feathered over her mouth. Jawid told me it was the custom of Muslim women to be modest in their demeanour and to conceal their mouths. When I did catch glimpses, I saw yellowed and twisted teeth. It was vanity, not the Koran, that kept her hand over her mouth, I decided.

I sat before her, watching her nibble at her hanky and feeling the black eyes of the beautiful woman with rotten teeth lingering over me, and I listened to her story.

"The Russians came," said Golbahar, "and brought their laws to us. I fought them." She started choking into her handkerchief until her face turned red. The young woman remained very still, watching only me.

"Are you all right?" I asked.

Golbahar nodded, wiped at her mouth and breathed deeply.

"The Russians," she said again, "brought their judges here and their prosecutors. They killed my boys. My clients, I mean, of course." She touched my arm as she said that. "Executions were too common. The constitution meant little to those judges. I actually beat them every time. Ate them up...!" And then she began to laugh, hard. The laugh became a cough and the cough became a choke. When she composed herself at last, she sat quietly for a moment, as though reviewing the damage caused by the latest outburst.

In the silence, I asked her, "So, you won many cases?" To that the young woman laughed.

"None," said Golbahar. "Of course."

Jawid nodded with her answer and looked embarrassed for me.

"Mr. Poudon," Golbahar said. "You are in Tajikistan ... not Canada. Here everyone is born guilty." I expected laughter with that. None came. Her eyes began to sparkle. "You become innocent only once in a lifetime," she said. "Do you know when that is?" She waited for an answer, eyes twinkling.

"Tell me," I said.

"When you become ... president, of course," she said, and with that she laughed and coughed and coughed and continued coughing for the rest of our brief interview, and as she walked out of my container and down the corridor to the main building, and through it, and into the street.

"Amazing," I said to Jawid when she had gone. "To speak in such a way."

Jawid's face was flushed and alight with a look I had not seen in him before this moment. "She is wonderful," was all he could say.

In the end, we did not choose Golbahar to represent us and protect our interests at the trial, though we should have. In my overly conservative lawyer's view I felt we needed a hardier, more robust body in that court, one that wasn't at risk of keeling over in a tubercular fit. I had believed, at that moment at least, that the legal process of the trial was real and that we would indeed have a role to play.

Some days later I finally met with the lawyer whom I would eventually choose. His name was Marlov, counsel for the other international agencies and one of the few we interviewed who did not seem to exaggerate his importance or his success. His price was $200 per day, an enormous wage by Tajik standards, but one the UN agreed to pay, so I didn't care. Negotiating the contract with him was straightforward, except for one clause: he wanted guaranteed asylum in the West after the trial, a request I could not grant.

"They may wish to kill me for this," Marlov said to me in a hushed voice in my container in the UN bunker one afternoon.

Comments like this were never lightly taken under such a regime as existed in Tajikistan. He was not exaggerating.

"Who will?" I asked.

He rubbed his hands together. "KGB or *mujaheds*," came the reply, through Jawid. Everyone still called the Tajik security apparatus the KGB, even though it was no longer linked to this former Soviet behemoth.

"KGB? Why the KGB?"

His role in the trial would be to represent the interests of the UN to ensure that a fair trial was conducted and the right parties found guilty. It was no more than that. "It will depend on who did this killing," he said.

"The KGB? Not the KGB. That would not be possible."

As the translation of what I said was filtered through to him, a smile crept up his face. "If you say so," he said.

"You think it could be possible?"

"Yes, why not?"

"There is no reason for the KGB, the government, to want these men dead. Is there?"

He pulled his metal chair over the metal container floor sounding like fingernails on a blackboard and ended up close enough to put his hand on my arm. Jawid's face was red.

"First, do not confuse the government with the KGB. They may be different on this matter. Next, you are probably right ... they may have no reason, but, who knows? Everything is possible. The KGB may have a reason that you may not think of. It may seem not logical, even crazy. That is the KGB." He slapped my arm and smiled. He looked at Jawid and gestured to me as he spoke.

Jawid said, "He says you look worried. Do not be worried. He says he is probably not right about the KGB, but he has to take care for possible problems." Jawid and the lawyer nodded at each other.

It was a disconcerting thought. Some of the UN staff had voiced opinions of government complicity in the killings, but these opinions seemed far-fetched and wrong. The theory was that the government wanted the KGB and international community aligned in a military campaign against the opposition and the mujahedeen and so orchestrated the killing of UN personnel. It made as much sense as any other conspiracy theory, and like most, was based on nothing more than fearful imaginations. However, hearing something similar from this Tajik lawyer gave me momentary pause. It was something to think about.

We could not agree to guarantee our lawyer's safety and resettlement in a Western country. We did agree, however, to undertake our best efforts with UNHCR, the UN's refugee agency, to obtain asylum for him outside Tajikistan, if the need arose. Content with this undertaking, lawyer Marlov signed the agreement.

My doubts about his safety and the role of government forces in the killings lingered, the latter fed by an opinion expressed by an Austrian police officer working for the UN who had been at the murder scene during the investigation while evidence was being collected by the Tajik police.

"Watching them, sometimes I had the feeling that it was just pretend," he wrote in his report.

There was good reason to concur with his conclusion. Throughout the course of the investigation, UN police had learned that a passenger bus had travelled on the same road as Team Garm at roughly the same time the killing had occurred. No effort had been made by the Tajik police to locate the driver or anyone on that bus.

Furthermore, a ridge overlooking the road held a Tajik military observation unit that had an unobstructed view of the entire road. At the time of the killings, the unit on duty was being rotated out and a new unit had yet to arrive. Allegedly by chance, the post was empty at the exact moment of the killings.

In their taped confessions, the accused stated they had taken hand-held radios from the victims. Each and every UN staff member is issued a hand-held radio. Phones were rare and a luxury and in the field, communication without these radios was impossible. Checking the inventory for the radios at UN HQ, I discovered that each of the hand-held radios of the dead men had been accounted for. The team had left them at the Garm station before they had set out on their trip that day. Yet, the confessions of the accused contained explicit reference to the radios. It was a strong indication to me that the confessions of the three men in custody had been scripted by their interrogators.

With my mind reeling with doubt as to the competence, motivation, and good faith of our Tajik partners, I enter the prison on the second day of the trial.

THE ACCUSED WILL SPEAK

(Dushanbe, Tajikistan—March, 1999)

We take our seats at school desks, the kind with a lone arm that ascends from a chair to a small surface for writing on. We are in the prison classroom, a narrow but long room with a blackboard lining the entire back wall. The three judges sit around the teacher's desk. This is the people's court, a panel of judges made up of one professional jurist and two laypersons, the Soviet judge and jury system combined into a single unit. Everyone is bundled in winter coats. The woman member of the court looks sad. Throughout the trial she will busily take notes on long, blank paper. It is the official transcript of what is said. The professional judge, presiding as the chief of the trial, paces behind the desk as we wait, or moves frequently between the classroom and the fire escape located just behind his desk to keep fresh tobacco in his lungs. I am surprised that smoking inside the court/classroom is prohibited.

Apart from the judges, there is the defence lawyer, the prosecutor, our counsel, Jawid, Jozef, and me in the court. Every other seat in the class is occupied by guards, in their long green winter coats, fur hats, and pale,

179

youthful faces. Every one of them seems to have bad skin. Each carries the standard-issue wooden truncheon.

An hour goes by without the trial commencing. Jozef, who has been smoking with the judge on the fire escape slides into the seat next to me and leans over. "I spoke with the judge outside," says Jozef. "He says he wants to finish the trial fast and convict them so we can go home."

"Great," I say. "Did he mean it?"

Jozef shrugs. "I suppose he did. Who knows for sure with these people?"

"He was joking, Jozef. He must have been joking. I hope he was joking. Was he joking?"

At that moment a large, grizzled, and much older version of the young guards walks in, looks at us, then steps aside and turns back to the door he has just entered. He is now facing the three prisoners who are walking single file into the room, young guards on either side. Wearing track pants and tops, the accused—Mirzo Muddin, Dovudov Saidrahman, and Darveshov Yoqub—enter the room appearing relaxed but confused, as if the holding of this trial is a complete surprise to them. Two have long hair and beards, one especially long, extending to at least below his sternum.

On one wall of the room hangs a painting of clowns dancing in a closed circle. I have been staring at it since we walked in. I assume some prisoner is the artist.

The prisoners stand by their chairs until told to sit. The senior guard nods and the three obediently sit in unison.

Once the prisoners are settled, the judge speaks. "Have you had a chance to speak with your lawyer?"

"No," says the one in the middle, with the longest beard. "We don't have a lawyer."

The judge immediately loses his temper. "Yes you do and you have seen him. Mr. Stajin is your lawyer. This man." The judge points and Stajin stands. The judge pulls his hand back and Stajin sits down.

The spokesman for the three says, "Okay. We have met him. Ten minutes. How can we prepare anything in ten minutes?"

The judge shouts at him, "Keep quiet! You are on trial for murder. Have some respect and talk only when talked to."

Through all of this, Jawid is alight with fascination. In his life he has never dreamed to be in such a place watching the two extremes of his country, the radical Muslims and the president's men, face off against each other in a court of law.

The charges are read to the men by the prosecutor, a tall, dark-haired man in a leather winter coat. He is dispassionate and aloof and not the same prosecutor we had met with previously. The three accused sit without expression. One constantly strokes the length of his beard. His nose is bent with an old break. Another, the youngest of the three, winks and smiles at the guards seated around him. They shake their heads at him, as friends would do to one another in mocking disbelief at some oafish misbehaviour.

With the charges formally read, the judge asks the defence lawyer if he is prepared to proceed. He answers that he has only been assigned the case one week before the trial and has met with his clients for just ten minutes. But he does not seem to be protesting the unfairness of the process.

"Now," the judge announces. "The accused will speak." In a Tajik trial, I learn, the accused are compellable, which means they are obligated to make a statement and to answer questions. There is no right to remain silent or presumption of innocence. Without investigative techniques or forensic evidence, the state relies on the words of an accused to prove its case. I ask myself what would happen if they refused to speak. I soon have my answer.

The judge is now yelling at them. "You must speak. If you do not speak, I will find you guilty and that is that."

Mirzo Muddin, the accused with the longest and darkest beard, announces that they will not talk in the court.

Jawid sits whispering his translations into my ear.

"Why should we say anything?" says Mirzo Muddin. "This is unfair procedure. We are innocent. Nothing more."

After translating the last sentence spoken, Jawid says to me, "He does not know what this trial is, I think."

The judge looks over to where Jozef and I sit, his face reddening in growing agitation. I can see his yellowed fingers fervently flipping through pages of some document.

"Look," he says, straining to keep his voice calm. "You must speak now. It is your chance to prove to us that you are innocent—"

"We are innocent—"

"Don't interrupt! You will have your chance. You will have a chance to say as much as you want. The United Nations is present to hear you." He points to us, and the accused look our way.

Mirzo Muddin then begins talking directly to me.

Before Jawid can translate, the judge slams his hand down. "Don't talk to them. Talk to the court."

Muddin stops and shakes his head. As he speaks, the judge grows enraged and begins shouting. Jawid has stopped translating, as though it is too much to repeat. I understand what is happening. Muddin continues to refuse to make a statement and the judge continues to lambaste him for it.

The three members of the people's court suddenly stand. The judge waves his arms and shouts. Jawid says, "They are stopping to let accused's lawyer speak with his clients. He must convince them to speak to the court. If they do not, the judge will continue with the case and convict them."

I had previously witnessed a number of temper tantrums acted out by various officials within totalitarian regimes. I developed a theory that in such governments the level of power achieved was directly proportional to how big and intimidating you were and how loud you could shout.

Our judge is a smallish man and so has been appointed a judge, one of the lowliest members of the pack's leadership. He can yell at you to make his point, but there is no danger of him beating you up.

The President of Tajikistan is a different type of figure. He is large and physically intimidating. I watched his style of governance first-hand at a sitting of Majlis-I-Oli, Tajikistan's parliament. The UN and diplomatic corps were the only ones permitted into the session to observe a number of bills ratified and turned into law, and to listen to the speeches and debates, such as they were. The session was subdued and calm, until the president lost his temper. His large, hulking frame sat at a wide desk up on a stage at one end of a cavernous, vaulted room, adorned with dark wood panels, desks, and a visitors' gallery tucked up and over the seats of the members of parliament. The proceedings began with the president seated in his tight-fitting grey suit, seemingly preoccupied by some document. Speaker after speaker came to the stage and spoke at the podium on any number of bills passing through the House. Watching each man take his turn was monotonous, routine, and boring.

The president finally stirred. A thin man with sharp features and wire eyeglasses was on his feet, talking about the new tax bill being proposed.

From what little of it I heard, he seemed to be the finance minister and he appeared to be describing how the government had agreed to a five-per-cent income tax reduction. Tajikistan lacked safe drinking water, warm schools, medicine, roads, and bridges. Yet here was this politician telling the country's representatives of a tax cut. The audience of elected men softly applauded and the thin man walked from the podium when the president slammed his open palm on his desk. "Ten per cent," he suddenly shouted. "Ten per cent."

The thin man stopped in mid-stride and whirled back to the podium. The cutting of percentages of taxes would presumably be a major event in a real body politic. Committees would be struck, hearings held, hard decisions made about programs to cut, programs to keep. Such a move could have profound and permanent effects on an economy, particularly one so sour and fragile as that in Tajikistan. I imagined that the lowering of taxes by five per cent had been studied extensively by the wisest of the country's financial soothsayers until they had agreed on the proactive effects of a five-per-cent shot to a withered economic arm.

But then, on a whim and with a hard slap of his hand on his presidential desk, the president had intervened and suddenly people were ten per cent richer, not five. A TV camera beside me blinked and whirred and the camera-man had his head buried at the end of the camera, watching through a small screen to ensure that no images of their president were lost. The feed was live, and flashed to Tajik households only in Dushanbe, the sole place in the country with a reasonably dependable supply of electricity.

The parliamentarians stood in applause for the president's bold and generous move. The camera blinked at him, then roamed over the officials on the floor. The man who had introduced the initial bill clapped too, but with less vigour than the rest. The five-per-cent additional cut seemed to have genuinely caught him off guard.

The business of the parliament then turned to a recent military conflict in the north, where members of a rebel force had entered Tajikistan from Uzbekistan. The rebels had reportedly taken over the airport in Khojund and shot up the town. They were driven out when the Tajik military arrived, after having ridden in like cavalry to the rescue.

With several pounding slaps of his palm against the wooden desk, the president lifted his giant's frame from his chair. The room vibrated with the sound and a hush descended. Out of the corner of my eye, I noticed the cameraman pull his head out from the camera and stand back. The red light that had been on throughout the session suddenly was out and the picture of the room that had been displayed on a small screen on the camera was black. The camera had been turned off. Strange, I thought.

The president then began loudly condemning those who had criticized the army by saying it had murdered and looted in the northern town they had purportedly come to save. He walked across the stage as he began this rant, a preacher chastising his congregation for daring to question a fundamental truth. Glaring at them, yelling, stomping, he used all of these gestures to make himself appear large and frightening. It worked—on me, at least.

He finally settled at the podium, at centre stage, and began a monotonous rampage of language. He shouted, he screamed, he turned red with his rage. Images of Hitler at the Reichstag came to mind. Here was the dictator archetype: a loud, mean, bully.

The president finally said what was really on his mind. For the first time in public, he denounced neighbouring Uzbekistan and its president. He accused some of those listening to him on the floor of Majlis-I-Oli of treason, treachery, and duplicity against the homeland. A hammer and sickle remnant hung on the wall behind him. The president then spoke of the territorial ambitions of Uzbekistan, its hegemony in the region, and its piracy of Tajik culture, land, cotton, and everything else. He shouted accusations against Uzbekistan, saying it was the Uzbek government behind the recent invasion and how if Uzbekistan wanted war, he would give it to them. I knew that that war, if it were to happen, would last as long as it took for Uzbekistan to move its giant military armada across the border. Uzbekistan had oil, electricity, and water, and, as a consequence, wealth. Tajikistan depended on its Uzbek cousin for power and would suffer greatly if it was turned off. And as I listened to the president's rant, I came to understand that I was watching a well-orchestrated play conducted by the president for the benefit of those in the house disloyal to him. He was telling them that he was not afraid of them, that he knew who they were, and that he would take his revenge. I felt the mood in the room change. One of those present, a young general of a particularly brutal military unit, and himself a young drug addict and drug dealer who rose to power on heroin, shouted back at the president. He referred to himself as a loyal servant of the state and challenged the president to accuse him outright. The president ignored the interruption and continued on.

After the session, waiting at the doors as the parliamentarians filed out, I saw in some faces looks of despair. Flushed cheeks, wide eyes, frenetic movement carrying them out and away, as fast as they could go. I wondered whether bodies would begin to be found over the coming days.

Against a mighty neighbour like Uzbekistan, also manhandled by a blunt and brutish dictator, the Tajik president could ill afford a direct and frontal challenge. He would be squashed flat. Yet needing to communicate fear, at the precise moment of the president's tirade, he had had the camera quietly turned off and the TV picture silenced. Tajiks sitting glued to their sets in Dushanbe lost their president. No recording of what he said existed, so in closed sessions with Uzbekistan he could deny the rumour of his accusations against his beloved cousin. Only the lowly parliamentarians heard first-hand this brazen act of defiance and threat.

Indeed, in news reporting the following day, little was said of this portion of the session. It was as though it had never happened.

Ah, to be a dictator for a day, yell at people, turn off TV cameras, and alter history.

PRISONS

(Dushanbe, Tajikistan—March 1999)
(Kingston, Ontario—May 1982)
(Phnom Penh, Cambodia—1992)

The sky is a crystal blue. One of those cloudless days in winter when everything appears sharpened by the cold and the ground feels brittle underfoot.

Jozef, the judge, and I stand on the fire escape off our classroom/court-room waiting for the defence lawyer to finish speaking with his clients. He is trying to convince them, we assume, to make opening statements to the people's court, as they are compelled by Tajik law to do. Speak now, he is telling them, or forever hold your head in your hands in some shallow grave in the prison yard.

I stare into that yard and beyond to the buildings housing the prisoners. No one from the Ministry of Justice could or would tell us how many prisoners were inside. The prison was a city administered by a governor who answered to no one. Intakes and releases were at his discretion alone, and he often ignored the orders of the few brave judges who fashioned habeas corpus-type orders for those finished their sentences or wrongly accused. I imagined the governor in a small room with a sloped roof and two piles of paper. "He stays," he would pronounce, picking out a slip and reading; "he goes," he would add, picking out another, laughing heartily to himself as he made his selections.

The first prison I had occasion to enter was Kingston Maximum Security Penitentiary in Kingston, Ontario. I entered through the ancient iron gates with a group of large and sullen men, moving in chain-gang slowness into the prison grounds. My first thought was of the large stone walls surrounding the inner yard and the sense of frustration in watching a seagull soaring back and forth over the wall. It was 1982 and I was trying out for the Ottawa Rough Riders, a professional football team. Training camp was held at Queen's University in Kingston and on an off day, a former player, Ron Stewart, then a Corrections Canada official, had offered us a tour. A handful of the players accepted.

It was in that prison that I met my first serial killer. I would meet many more in the future: Khmer Rouge soldiers and officers; the Tajikistan leadership; members of Cambodia's secret police. But here was my first. We were being taken down an isolation wing of the prison that housed, in protective custody, sex offenders and snitches and anyone else deemed at risk from the crooked arm of prison justice. We had just come through the old wing, now abandoned, but never fully repaired from a prison riot some years earlier, when the guards had evacuated in the face of a surge of violence and mayhem and had locked those in protective custody in their cells, to protect them from their fellow inmates. Prisoners from the general prison population had broken into the protective custody zone with the guards now out of the prison, and had used crowbars to open the individual cells of the stool pigeons and the pedophiles and the rapists, and had exacted ferocious and misguided justice on them. The bent cell bars remained the testament to the acts of cruelty carried out in a Canadian prison that day.

In the newer wing, the cells were full. I straggled behind our group, fascinated by the smallness of the cells and the lives lived inside them. I lingered over each tiny room.

"We are animals in a zoo," one of the inmates suddenly called out to me as I walked by his cell. He approached the bars from the back of his cell.

He was a thin, pale man, with the pasty, unhealthy complexion of someone living constantly indoors. One full wall of his four-by-eight-foot cell was covered with photographs of naked women.

"Ah, I don't mind," he said, seeing that he had embarrassed me. "You're with those football players."

"Yes," I said, not knowing whether I should be talking to him or not.

"You seem small for a football player. Skinny. Fast, are you?"

"Fast," I said.

The other players had seen me in conversation and were slowly making their way back to where I stood. Windows lined the wall outside the prisoner's cell, but they were located too high up on the wall to see anything but sky.

The prisoner pulled out a letter he had written and showed it to me. "Take this, read it. What has happened to me isn't fair. I wrote to the Minister of Justice."

He saw my hesitation. "Oh, don't worry. I won't bite ya." The other players had now grouped around the cell. "Hello fellows," he said. No one returned the greeting. He showed them the letter and began reading from it. He had been promised $10,000 per victim for his co-operation in advising police where he had hidden the bodies of the girls he had killed in British Columbia. The Minister of Justice had not yet paid him and he was writing to complain and to demand payment. His family needed it to survive, he said. I couldn't recognize the man's face from any press I had seen, so I stepped away from the cell to read his nameplate, positioned over the cell door. Clifford Olson. I knew this name, had seen his face in a newspaper photograph taken as he was leaving court for a prison van to begin his life behind bars. That was several years before. He had murdered children between the ages of nine and eighteen in British Columbia in the early 1980s, and been convicted for eleven of those murders. I stared at him, at the wall of breasts, at his letter. From within the safety and security of our society, this monster had emerged.

I would often unintentionally return to that thought and to that gaunt but lively face staring back at me in Kingston Pen, whenever I was confronted with images of the wanton inhumanity visited upon victims in a war, an after-war, an ethnic cleansing. No culture is immune from hatching monsters.

My first exposure to Third World prisons was in Cambodia. With free access to these facilities granted us under the Peace Accord, we pushed our way in through the front door of Phnom Penh Central Prison, passed young boy guards who carried no weapons but strode across the grounds holding each other's hands or locked arm in arm.

The smell of mould and rot inside the barrack walls competed with that of urine and feces. One hundred men or more shared a long dark building, sleeping on mats laid out over a concrete slab. The men slept in two rows, facing one another, fifty to a row. At night, they would lie down on the slab and have a metal semicircular bracelet placed around each ankle. A long steel rod was then slid through islets in the open part of each bracelet and attached at the end of the slab to a lock embedded in the concrete. In this way, the men were locked down for the night, attached to one another, unable to change position. Most lay on their backs, staring straight up, linked with fellows on either side, in forty-degree-Celsius heat. Walking into that barracks room was like walking into a human oven. When we arrived, a few prisoners, those too ill to move, were lying on the concrete. Most others were in the barracks standing, squatting, working at sweeping, or scrubbing. It was in the interest of their own survival that the place be kept clean.

Outside, we found isolation cells for prisoners under punishment. These were individual cells in rooms the size of closets in which prisoners were kept shackled twenty-four hours per day. One saw me through a narrow opening in the steel door and, placing his hands together in a prayer sign, begged for help. The shock of what I was seeing left me speechless and, as always, angry at these acts of inhumanity.

Inhumanity. A separate building sat off to one side in the prison compound. It was padlocked. We need to see inside, we said.

You cannot, we were told.

We insisted.

The guard with the key has gone home for lunch.

We will wait, we said. And we did. We waited for hours before a guard arrived with a ring of keys. Someone had finally gone to get him. He apologized and seemed sincere. We thanked him and he unlocked the door. The building was a French colonial structure, resembling a villa with columns and a balcony and shutters on the windows. Inside, the ground floor was empty.

"Anything upstairs?" I asked the guard. He shrugged. We climbed a narrow staircase at the back of the villa and opened a door at the top of the stairs to a small corridor with two doors on either side. I tried the doors. They were locked.

"The key, please," I said to the guard. Without question he quickly moved to unlock the first door and in we stepped. It was 2 p.m. and my shirt was soaked with sweat.

Kiempo, my interpreter, saw what was inside first. The room we were in was bare. Along one of the walls, a few feet up from the floor and only on a part of the wall, a line of metal bars separated the room from another room, one that was dark and seemed at first to be some kind of storage area, sunk three or four feet lower than the room we stood in. But then we saw the men. Heads bobbed up to look at us and hands gripped the bars. Men were in this storage room, looking up at us through the bars.

My first question was: "How did you get in there?" They pointed to a second door in the room, which opened to a hallway leading to stairs down to the subfloor they were kept on.

"Who are you?" I asked.

"Political prisoners," said Kiempo, translating.

As it turned out, they were members of the Funcinpec political party. Some had been reported missing by their party and we had, in fact, been looking for them.

"I want these men released," I told the boy guard.

Kiempo laughed as he repeated and translated the reply. "He says: 'Tell it to my boss, sir.'"

Another closed door stood at the end of this sub-hallway. "What is in there?" I asked. The guard pushed the key in and smiled. Opening the door, we walked into a well-lit and spacious room, a sharp contrast to the dark and moist rooms we had just been through. I squinted into the light and saw a large man lying on an army cot by the window. He was drenched in sweat and naked except for his red cotton underwear, and as we entered his room he sat up to reveal how large he was, a giant in fact, possibly six-foot-five or taller. His giant's feet spread out like planks on the floor. His face had a slight deformity to it that made it look crooked and frightening. His skin colour was white as snow, with bright red suntan bands along his arms and neck.

"Hello," he said in English. My thirsty mouth hung open in disbelief. He remained seated on his cot; a small bowl of fruit lay on a table next to him.

"What is this?" I said to no one.

"A giant!" said Kiempo quickly.

I looked back at the guard. He smiled at me.

"Who are you?" I asked the giant.

"Yes, well. My name is Leo," said the giant. "Come in, have some fruit. Can you help me? They are keeping me here."

"Why?" I asked.

"I do not know. Please can you tell my embassy? I am German. I need to be out of here."

In this decrepit French villa, under lock and keys kept by a guard who went home for lunch, a giant German tourist was being held prisoner in a room adjacent to Cambodian political detainees. I had seen the shackles outside, now this.

"I will speak with the head of the prison," I said, trying not to stare at his deformed face, "and get you out of here." I assumed that he had been arrested under some pretext in order to extract payments, although the fruit and the breezy, light-filled room seemed wrong, somehow.

"Thank you," said the giant, and lay back down on his cot.

I turned to the guard. "We need to see your commander," I said.

"He is not in the prison today," came the reply.

"Well, who is in charge?"

His young face blushed. "I am," he said. He could not have been older than eighteen.

I knew that talking to this young man would not get me anywhere. I finally convinced the guard to send for the prison commander, also at home at lunch, and by now, asleep. We left the building and waited in his office for him to come. A member of the Ghanaian UN police detachment remained outside the giant's cell, in case an attempt was made to sneak him and the political prisoners away before a political storm arose. We needn't have worried.

The commander looked half-asleep when he finally arrived. He sat silently listening to our complaints over the shackling, the political prisoners, and the giant. The use of shackles was contrary to international law, we told him, and now contrary to Cambodian law with the passage of a UN written criminal code.

He nodded. The German was a tourist arrested by UN military in Siem Reap for stealing antiquities from the temples there, he told us. He was transferred to Phnom Penh to be close to his embassy, members of whom had been in the prison on frequent visits to him, bringing fruit. "I wanted to just let him go," said the commander, "but the Germans and UNTAC insisted we detain him. So here he is."

I don't know why I'm here, said the German. The lying sack of shit.

The commander continued. "The Funcinpec men are petty criminals. But, if you say I should release them, I will." I felt flushed with embarrassment. The issue of the shackles remained, on that matter at least I was on high ground.

"Well," he began calmly, "the fact is the lock on our front gate is broken and most of the guards go home at night. We have little choice. The men in shackles now are murderers and my guards cannot handle them. Tell me what I should do."

In other prisons in the country we would encounter prison guard sadists lighting prisoners on fire and splitting open their toes or backs with punishing blows from hammers and bamboo whips. This one was not such a man.

Over the next days we raised the issue of the shackles at the highest levels and exacted promises of reform. When it didn't happen, human rights officers entered the prison and ripped the shackles out of the walls. I have one of the shackles taken from that prison on my desk. The Funcinpec prisoners were indeed petty criminals, but we had them released just the same as a gesture to Prince Sihanouk and his son; Funcinpeckers, we called them, for their constant whining.

We were told that the German giant was returned home to Germany.

I would never see inside the prison living quarters in Tajikistan, but as we stand in the cold waiting to resume the trial, I watch as a prisoner enters the yard from the cells for what appears to be a period of exercise. He is surrounded by four guards. The guards take him into the centre and then back away to the four corners of the yard and turn to watch him. Starting slowly with swings of his arms the prisoner begins what looks like jumping jacks. However, as I watch I quickly realize he is dancing—hip hop dancing. One foot, then the other and then a shuffle of his feet and then he is off in a frenetic, athletic dance. He spins on one foot and kicks high in the air and moonwalks on that spot in the middle of the prison yard. We watch him, spellbound by his energy and skill, for the longest time.

"Sir, the lawyer is ready," Jawid comes out to tell us. Reluctantly, I turn away from the dancer down below and head back into the court.

READY TO TALK
(Dushanbe, Tajikistan—March, 1999)

When the accused stand to give their testimony in the trial in Dushan-be, I am struck by the importance of this moment, where I am, and who these men are. Muslim fundamentalists had allegedly murdered four UN peacekeepers. A religiously moderate Muslim judge would adjudicate on their guilt. Everyone presumed them to be guilty. What would the men say in their defence?

Our judge barks out at them, "Ready to talk?"

The men sitting opposite me had killed before, of that there was no doubt. They were soldiers in the war against the Russians and the army from Du-shanbe. They had fled into Afghanistan or gone higher into the Pamir moun-tains. They had grown up living with a pack of men who depended on one another to stay alive. Loyalty was burned deep into their psyches. Without the pack, they would not be alive.

Their experiences of life are so far beyond my own that I feel slightly uncomfortable being here, being part of a system standing in judgment of them. My lawyer's credentials, my UN passport, my suit hardly give me au-thority over what has happened in the harsh domain of their lives.

195

A general may have given them an order which they obediently carried out. Now, they are on trial for their lives.

But what order, if any, did they carry out?

Mirzo Muddin rises, prayer beads in hand, to begin his statement.

"I am innocent of these crimes," he begins by saying. "I would never harm UN people. I am Muslim and therefore do not kill innocents. It is against the Koran."

The Muslim judge pounds his desk, pointing his finger at him and angrily denounces what he has just heard. "Don't give us this garbage," he says. "You and your fighters in Afghanistan, you *mujaheds*, have killed plenty of innocent people. Don't try to tell these UN people sitting here and the families of the men who died that you would not kill innocents because you are Muslim."

"It is true," says Mirzo Muddin.

"Silence," says the judge. "You can speak now but only about the crime."

"I am telling of this."

"We don't want to hear lies. Now, continue."

Muddin looks down at his prayer beads, rolling them between his fingers like someone rolling a cigarette. He is silent for several minutes and I expect the judge to scream at him again. He doesn't, and Muddin continues.

"We were ordered by our field commanders, Mullo Abdullo and Mirzo Zoev, to travel to Dushanbe from Qarategin to be questioned. We followed our orders."

That fact alone is astonishing to hear. Such is their pack loyalty that they would come down from the safety of their mountains to give themselves up to an enemy they had come to despise and fear in order to allow themselves to be questioned by the Ministry of Interior (MOI), renowned for its use of torture.

Into the hands of torturers these foot soldiers delivered themselves, because the leaders of the pack needed them to. The international presence in Tajikistan, for all its defects, incompetence, and misunderstandings, had created a buffer between the opposition and the government to allow a semblance of calm to return to their country. The opposition leadership in Dushanbe, although wary and insecure, were not being hunted down daily. The absence of war allowed them to come out of caves and other isolated mountain hiding places. They needed peace—for themselves, for their families, for their people. Consequently, they needed the UN to broker that peace. When the Garm team had been murdered, and the UN had pulled out of the Qarategin valley and retreated to Dushanbe, the possibilities for peace diminished. Whoever had been responsible for the killing in the Qarategin valley—and an opposition field commander was certainly behind it—guilty persons had to be found and given up. The three men sitting in front of us had been chosen to play the part of the guilty—or perhaps, they may have been.

"Mullo Abdullo told me that we would stay in Dushanbe for only one day and then return home," Muddin says. "I do not understand what has happened, why I am here now. I should be at home ... I have a wife...." Head bent, he vigorously worries his prayer beads.

"We were taken to the KGB offices and put in separate rooms. At first, two men were in the room with me. I was asked if I had killed the UN people. I said no. I was slapped in the face and asked again. I said no. A third man entered, a large man. His name I have learned. It was Sasha. He began punching me in the face. I tried defending myself. He punched me hard, broke my nose." He runs a finger over the ridge of inverted cartilage on his nose, the same evidence of a break, though less fresh, that I had seen on his taped confession.

"I was beaten for a long time. I would not confess to a crime I did not do. They brought me to a different room. I was strapped to a table. They put wires on my legs and arms ... They gave me electricity...." And all at once Mirzo Muddin begins to sob, shoulders violently shaking with the intensity of his crying, the only sound in the room. Everything is being released, memories of his torture, perhaps, his fears for the present, his longings to be home and the betrayal, which he must now finally feel. This spectacle of a man crying, particularly with such force, is almost unbearable to watch. Even the judge seems affected.

"Sit down," he says gently.

Muddin sits. The two other accused keep their heads rigidly down, chin to chest. The young guards stare at Muddin, scarcely believing what they have seen, a man such as this, crying. On the people's court, the woman dabs at the corner of her eye. Jawid's mouth hangs open. It is as though the Pamir mountains themselves are weeping.

"Compose yourself," says the judge. "This is not helping you."

Muddin continues crying, but silently now. We sit in silence, watching, not watching him, feeling pity for this man.

Wiping an open palm over his face, he slowly stands once again.

"Continue," says the judge.

"They brought me a paper with a story written on it ... The story said that I had killed the UN people. They stopped the electricity. They told me to sign the paper or they would turn the electricity back on ... The pain was great ... I signed to stop the pain."

He hangs his head again and I think he will start to cry once more. The judge quickly asks him, "Is that all you have to say?" Without waiting for an answer, the judge turns to the defence lawyer, who appears to be trying to remain unseen and unheard. The judge asks him if he has any questions for his client. Reluctantly, the defence lawyer rises and then asks the question I would have asked. "Where were you at the time of the killing?"

"What time was the killing?" asks Muddin.

The lawyer shuffles through his papers. "Well," he says, "I'm not sure...."

We prompt our lawyer to speak up. He stands quickly and says, "Between 2 and 4 p.m., July 20."

Muddin looks across at us and speaks to us. "I was in the Dharban district and then Komsomolobad for the entire day. I was with my wife and then others. I can name all who saw me in that afternoon." Muddin then lists by name a number of people who had seen him in those districts.

"Sit down," says the judge after Muddin has finished. "Next."

The two others stand in turn and tell their stories of torture and of following orders, and of being innocent.

"We will stop for today," the judge announces after the accused have finished their statements, "and start again on Monday. Goodbye."

It is 1 p.m. The trial of the men accused of killing Team Garm has concluded its first day of evidence.

MINISTRY OF INTERIOR
(Dushanbe, Tajikistan—March, 1999)

Some months before I arrived in Tajikistan, a French couple working for an NGO aid agency was kidnapped off the streets of Dushanbe and held for ransom. Banks in Tajikistan held little cash and any local currency on hand was usually devalued within hours of leaving the vaults. Gold was not readily available, and though gems were mined in the country, they were quickly taken out. One of the few commodities left of value was the warm body of a hostage. Kidnapping had become commonplace and very deadly, sometimes because of police and army bungling, but sometimes because, with nothing left to trade, the families of the kidnapped watched helplessly until a body was found on a street.

Regrettably for the NGO couple, the government tracked them down, God knows how, and sent soldiers in guns blazing. The woman died of her wounds, but the man made it out alive to tell the tale of the military's blundering. The bullets that had killed his girlfriend had come from the military, not the kidnappers.

With this history of the region in mind, I initially rationalized the killing of the UN Team Garm as an aborted and tragic end to a kidnap attempt. No value was gained, I believed, from the dead bodies, when live ones would bring a price.

But rational thought often has no place in the rhythm and reason of war and postwar. Loyalty is sacrosanct when everything else is dissolving. As I sit watching the three accused in their classroom desks on Monday morning of the second true day of the trial, I know these men had done exactly as they were told. That is self-evident. They had been told to come to Dushanbe by their leadership and hand themselves over to an enemy they did not trust and continued to fear. That simple act took an iron-willed belief that those who gave the order would protect them.

If they had been told to kill the UN men at Garm, they would have done so without question. The only issue that remained was whether they had indeed received that order.

The prosecutor stands and calls his first witness. It is an officer from the Ministry of Interior. He had questioned the accused and, according to him, elicited confessions through his questioning.

The prosecutor asks, with high drama. "Did you lay a hand on these men?"

"Never," the witness answers quickly, lowering his head as he opens and then closes his winter coat. "We tricked them into answering."

The defence lawyer for the men rises to say he has no questions and I know the fix is on.

I prod our lawyer, Marlov. He nods to me and stands.

He asks, "How long did you question these men?"

"I don't remember."

"How many of you questioned them?"

"I don't know. A few."

"Who ordered you to do the questioning?"

"I don't remember."

"Why is it that one of these men appears on video with a broken nose? Did he have a broken nose when he came to you?"

"Not sure."

"You and your men broke his nose."

"No."

Marlov then hesitates. The way he is standing when he questions the witness blocks my view of the prosecutor, who sits behind a table in line with ours. The first indication that something is wrong comes when our lawyer turns to me, his face suddenly red. He then looks back to the judge and says he has no further questions. I am outraged that he has stopped and I move closer to tell Jawid to tell him to get back on his feet. Jawid holds up his hand to me as he leans in to listen to what Marlov is telling him. Then Jawid turns to me and says, "Lawyer says he has been threatened. Prosecutor has signalled him to stop questioning. So he has stopped."

"Signal ... what signal? What is he talking about?"

"I saw also," says Jawid. "He used his finger ... over his throat. I cannot show."

But as soon as Jawid says the words I know it is true. Marlov's face had said it to me as it turned red and he became suddenly uncertain. He had been directed to stop, and he obeyed. He had to live in Tajikistan well after the trial had ended, and we didn't.

I think for a moment of raising it with the judge or of using other political means to allow our lawyer unrestrained freedom in the court. But I am mindful of the consequences for him, and for the prosecutor. You never know who will suffer the blame in this society. In fact, we can live with the unanswered questions from the Ministry of Interior. We know the men have been tortured into confessions so we need not push any further. The real question is, given that the confessions are unreliable, did these men commit the crimes nonetheless?

There is one witness I am anxious to hear. She is a twelve-year-old Tajik girl from the Komsomolobad area who was on the very road the day of the killing and had said, in her signed statement, that she saw the UN vehicle on the road being chased down by a red car with three men in it. The importance of this testimony is the circumstantial confirmation of the colour red and the number three. Mirzo Muddin's vehicle is red in colour. And, of course, three men are on trial for the murder.

"She speaks no Russian," Jawid says to me, translating the discussion that is then taking place between the judge and prosecutor. "We will need a Tajik interpreter because the court must be done in Russian."

"Great. More delays."

"No. Wait. They have someone. She is outside. They have asked her to come and she agrees. They will bring her in."

One of the boy guards is already moving across the room to the doorway across from where we sit. He returns with a woman I know, the woman with bad teeth and beautiful hair and eyes, the lawyer who had arched her eyebrow at me and had brought the queen to me. She walks in without a glance at us and takes her place beside the girl sitting in the makeshift witness box at the front of the court.

The girl wears a *rumoli* headscarf and a dress with the same floral pattern I have seen on every dress on every ethnic Tajik woman in the country. She seems very afraid and speaks haltingly, nervously.

The woman lawyer translates what the girl has said. "She says she saw a red car chasing the UN car. She says she did not see the shooting, but heard later. She was on the road carrying something. What were you carrying?" She leans to the girl, who speaks in a very soft voice with her head down.

"Water, it sounds like. But I am not sure. Her accent is very strong and she speaks in a very simple way."

Jozef turns to our lawyer before he is set to ask his questions for us. "Take this scarf," says Jozef, taking the red scarf from around his neck. "Ask her what colour this is?"

The lawyer stands. He asks the girl if she knows her colours. She says yes. He then produces the scarf.

"What is this colour?" he asks gently.

The woman asks the question of her and when the girl does not answer she asks again. The judge then speaks to her and the woman speaks to the girl again.

Finally, the woman looks out at us, but speaks to me. "She does not know the colour red. She cannot identify this colour as red."

The judge has a deep scowl on his face.

"Ask her if she knows it by another name." I say to our lawyer.

The question is asked.

"No," says the woman. "I think she does not know colours."

Our lawyer then points around the room, at the paintings, the stripes on the accused's pants, at anything with shades of red. What are these colours, she is asked. She does not know, comes the reply.

Finally, gently, our lawyer poses the question. "How could you know the colour of the car was red?"

The judge interrupts. "He says that is enough," Jawid translates for us. "No more questions."

The end of the second day and the prosecution closes its case. Confessions true or false, but beaten out of the accused. A twelve-year-old girl told what to say. No ballistics or forensics of any kind. The defence lawyer then stands and tells the judge his intention of calling a dozen or so witnesses to corroborate the accused's alibi of where they were when the killing happened. He has a list of names he is prepared to hand up to the court. The judge waves him off.

Jawid looks at me and then back at the two men. Jozef says, "No, this can't be."

I am out of the language loop and nudge Jawid. "What is it, Jawid? Jozef?" I did understand the anger of the defence lawyer; his voice is raised and he seems pale. Our own lawyer is shaking his head.

Finally, Jawid turns back to me. "Judge say no. No defence witness can be called. Denied."

"What is this?" I ask. "That's wrong. How can it be?"

The defence lawyer then proceeds to argue for the removal of the trial judge on grounds of bias.

"Denied," says the judge. "Tomorrow at 9:30 for final statements from the lawyers." He bangs his fist on the table and walks quickly out of the court. We watch him, frozen by the moment that has just occurred. Even the prosecutor seems caught off guard.

"Jozef," I say. "Go speak with him. Smoke with him. Explain that this is not right."

"The decision's made," says Jozef. "Can't you see? But I go, I go."

I look over at the three accused, all staring straight at me. "Jawid. Tell these men I will not let this happen. It is wrong."

Jawid stands to walk over to the men but the guards are on their feet and then the men are on their feet and being led out of the court. He doesn't get the chance.

I can think of no rational reason why the judge can possibly make the order he has. Even if the trial is a sham, why not pretend, hear the witnesses, and then convict the accused? What the judge has now done is somehow worse, more a display of contempt for the process and for our concerns of fairness. Obviously, no one cares what we think. The judge has been told to end the trial quickly and the prospect of a stream of defence witnesses has threatened to delay the inevitable.

I am determined not to allow this to happen. I will take it up with the UN special representative, Jan Kubis, ask him to speak with the president if he has to.

As I collect my notes from on top of the school desk where I sat watching the spectacle, the wife of the UN interpreter killed in the Garm ambush approaches me. She has been present for both days of the trial and has heard everything we heard.

"Hello, sir," she says in English.

"Hello, Mrs. Mahramov. Sorry for this. How are you?" I guess that she will ask me once more about the death benefits still not paid to her by the UN. It is a lingering embarrassment for us, I believe.

"I am fine, sir," she says. "I am fine." She hesitates, as though still debating whether she should speak to me or not. She finally decides. "Sir, I have listened to the stories. At first I thought these boys innocent of the crimes. They have been tortured. The police have lied. The little girl has been made to speak, it seems. My heart was heavy with this. But today ... today I change my mind." Her eyes well with tears and she wipes at a corner.

"Tell me," I say, sitting back down.

"Today, at lunch, I was walking from the prison and from across the road the family of one, Muddin, I think, came to me. It was his mother and his aunt. They say, sorry for what my son has done. He is good boy. He made mistake. Sorry. I accepted what they say, then I think to myself why say such things if not really guilty. They were saying sorry to me. They were saying he is killer. I think now ... he did crime. His family know he was not home, as he say he was. He is killer, sir, and must be punished." Her lip is trembling.

I open my hands. "I have no power here," I say. "Guilty or not, the judge will decide."

"No. No. Of course, I not ask for anything else. I am just telling. These men are killers. Goodbye, sir."

"Goodbye, Mrs. Mahramov." I stand as she leaves, and think of her husband sitting in that car on that road, a road he knew so well and a people he understood. He saw them coming and must have known what was to happen. Maybe his killers had been caught and maybe they would indeed be punished. But the process we were now in was not about justice for anyone, and that was what worried me most.

TAJIKS WILL NOT KILL TAJIKS
(Dushanbe, Tajikistan—March 1999)

Jozef, Jawid, and I return to the UN offices looking for Kubis, discover him to be out of the country, and so we speak with Bhatia, his number two.

Lip extended in his perpetual pout, Bhatia listens intently to what has just happened.

He asks me, "What do you think must be done?"

"Well, we cannot directly interfere with the court. But we need to remind whoever is behind this *court* of the need for an impartial and fair trial. We will not sanction it without it."

Bhatia nods. "It is a serious matter, no doubt. But, Ronald, what does the government care about our sanctioning it or not?"

"If we say this trial is unfair, and do not approve the outcome ... we will not send our people back into the field. We will never be sure of safety. If not in the field, we cannot monitor the peace process and we cannot approve of elections."

His eyes widen considerably as he listens to what I have to say, then nods vigorously. He stirs his tea. "Right. If we cannot send people out, and, as you say, cannot monitor the election ... who do you suppose this benefits?"

"You're not saying this is some kind of conspiracy to keep us in Dushanbe—"

"No. No. No. Of course not. But you are speaking now of their concern for our sanction. They will not be concerned. Don't misunderstand. I am not saying we should not take this seriously. But don't be disappointed, that's all."

I had seen Tajikistan's president at work and knew him to be a dictator. It was his government controlling the police and military and, with the exception of Leninobod in the north, which remained always an uncertainty, the officials outside Dushanbe. The president would ensure his own victory in an election and the fewer international observers to monitor how he accomplished that, the better.

"What about international aid. The donors—the World Bank—have said that aid would not flow unless justice was done in this case and the killers brought to justice. Surely, the government will be concerned over dollars."

Again his eyes widen and he begins rummaging in a folder on his desk. He smiles. "Yes. True. They *were* concerned. After the murders, announcements were made. Concern expressed. The usual political-speak. Now.... Ah, here it is." He pulls out a sheet of paper and hands it to me. "You will read the latest World Bank pledge in the left column. In the right, the donors." I look down at the black-and-white confirmation of what Bhatia says, the money is returning.

"In international politics," Bhatia continued, "maybe all politics, there are moments of time when a matter is of concern. Once that moment has gone, it is gone forever. Garm is over, for them. No, the money is not a concern."

"Then, what do we have? What can move them?"

"An inherent need to do the right thing. To do justice, if they are so inclined. Don't forget, they are not now under some rock. You, Jozef, and Jawid are there on behalf of the community of nations. We are watching them, judging their conduct. That is not inconsequential. I will take this up, write to the Minister of Justice and express our hope that fair process be followed."

I feel deflated. "It must be sent today. The trial may end tomorrow."

"Yes, of course. Immediately. I will show you a draft when I have it finished."

"They have the death penalty here," I say.

He waves at me. "Don't worry. Tajiks won't kill Tajiks over this. They will not be killed. The worst will be that they are kept a short while in prison and then quietly released. Everyone will have what they want."

Tajiks have been killing Tajiks by the thousands for some years, I think to myself. I fail to see why that should change now.

Early the next morning, I am driving to a meeting with the chief justice of the Tajik Supreme Court and thinking about the purpose of my summons. I had been summoned by a government minister once before, in Cambodia. After a night out to dinner with an aid to the minister of security, during which we had a long discussion about the future of his country over Mekong sweet whisky, the minister sent me an invitation for talks with him, as though I had said something profound over dinner the night before and the minister himself decided he had to hear it directly from the source. A chance for such influence on a ministry that was so acutely engaged in human rights violations was too great an opportunity to pass up. The problem was, I couldn't remember what I had said at dinner that sounded intelligible enough to warrant such an audience. When we met, I had nothing terribly insightful to say to the minister other than "Don't torture or shackle or detain people without legal grounds." That kind of thing. We talked politely for an hour and I was then ushered out. As I left the building I thought I could hear his lieutenant being flogged for wasting his time. A despotic ruler doesn't need a lecture from an occidental human rights lawyer. He needs solutions to his main concerns. In Cambodia he wanted to know how, without forensic investigative tools, he and his men could obtain evidence of a crime. He wanted to know how to keep prisoners from escaping their sieve-like prisons without chaining them at night. He wanted to know how to hold someone they were investigating when they knew they had little more than a suspicion of guilt. I had no money for him and so no solutions for his problems. Platitudes were little more than an annoyance.

I think about this lesson as I drive with Jozef and Jawid to our meeting with the chief justice of the Supreme Court of Tajikistan and am determined not to engage in an empty lecture about fair process and natural justice.

The chief justice is a barrel-chested man, over six feet tall, with a booming voice and a face and demeanour that bears a striking resemblance to that of the president. It occurs to me that he may be a relative of the head of state, given a plum job for hacking off a head or two on his behalf. He encircles my hand and crushes it, sits us down at a long conference table in his office, and then serves us the best tea I have ever tasted. Jozef and I drink several cups. "This is delicious tea," Jozef keeps saying. I think for a moment that we have been drugged.

The discussions begin with his telling us he received the letter from Bhatia and now wants to hear from us what the problem is. Before we can answer, the door opens and several other men walk in, followed by the trial judge himself. The men are not introduced to us, which in itself I find strange. They take up seats around the table.

"This may not be appropriate to discuss in the presence of the judge," I say through Jawid.

"Don't worry. You don't mind, do you?" the chief says to the trial judge. He seems to have missed the point.

The judge shakes his head. "No," he says.

"Good. Now, what is the problem?"

"I can't talk in front of the judge," I say. "It is improper. The defence is not here."

"I am the chief judge and I will allow it. Now talk to us of the problem and we will see about a solution." He takes a loud slurp from his tea.

Jozef has finished his and is reaching for more. "I can't believe how good this is," he keeps repeating. He places a hand on my arm and says, "Try more tea ... And let us discuss things with them. Don't be too technical." Jozef is right, the opportunity for a moment with this chief judge cannot be missed. We will convince him of the requirement for a balanced and equitable trial. Clearly, not permitting any defence witnesses to speak is wrong. I decide to continue.

I explain first that the court is an independent body and we cannot intervene in its processes, that it must be left to make its own decision. Everyone in the room nods. I then praise the trial judge for his patience, being always cognizant of any punishment that may be meted out to an official we too openly criticize, and begin to outline the problem. I ask how, without hearing from the defence witnesses, the judge can have a complete picture of the facts. In addition, justice must be done, but it also must be seen to be done.

The public perception of a ruling excluding one side of a case will lead to the loss of further faith in the country's system of justice.

"I thought the men had confessed," says the chief justice suddenly.

"Yes. But there is a question of whether the confessions were true or not, given that they may have been tortured."

Over the two hours or so we spend together I engage him in discussions, uncomfortably balancing the need to respect the independence of the trial judge in matters related to the trial, and the equally strong need to ensure that the accused will receive a full and fair day in court.

The chief listens, asks a few more questions and then stands. "I understand now," he says. "I assure you the trial will be fair and meet all your expectations."

We all stand and shake hands.

As we drive away I feel self-satisfied and important. I am in Central Asia working as a lawyer for the United Nations. I have just intervened to ensure the court process for the three men on trial for their lives is conducted in a fair and open way.

Feeling smug, I ask Jozef as we drive from the office of the chief justice, "What do you think?"

"Not sure. I fear nothing will change. Sorry to say. But...." He pauses as he veers the Land Cruiser around a woman who had stepped off the curb without looking in our direction.

"Crazy people." He rolls down the window and shouts at her.

He then returns to his silent concentration on the road.

Surprised and impatient for him to finish what he has started, I prod. "But ... but what?"

He turns his head and looks at me. "But. The tea was very good. The best I have had."

Then he starts to laugh.

"Thanks," I say.

"Welcome."

DEATH . . . FOR EACH ONE
(Dushanbe, Tajikistan—March 1999)

Dushanbe is a jewel that sparkles in the bright sunlight. Over and around it a clear blue sky is interrupted only by the white outlines of snow-dusted mountains.

The day is warm and I am enjoying the hot sun on my face as we wait outside the prison for the judge to arrive. The defence lawyer, someone I had early on wrongly dismissed as being a party to a quick and meaningless trial process, approaches me. My newfound respect for him has arisen from the vigour with which he had asked the judge to withdraw from the trial on grounds of bias. He now wants to know what we did about his request to call witnesses. I outline the details of the meeting with the chief justice, how I believe that meeting to have been improper but how I also believe it has achieved the desired result.

"Will I have my witnesses?" he asks me.

"I am certain you will."

The atmosphere around the prison has changed. The soldiers are no longer present and the prison and court officials seem more animated. Something has happened. Something we know nothing about. Outside the prison in the bright morning of a mountain sky, I sense a resolution has been reached.

And then the trial process becomes even more curious.

The courtroom is crowded with families of the accused, political types, and a TV camera. For this day, the proceedings will be seen throughout Tajikistan.

Finally the judge enters and we stand. His first words leave me hollow and in shock.

"The defence request is denied. Begin your statements."

As he stands, the defence lawyer looks back at me, but with little hesitation begins his plea of innocence. He speaks for no more than ten minutes. The prosecutor stands next and reviews the confessions in detail. In a voice without passion he simply says, "They are guilty."

The judge calls for a recess and we are again on our feet.

"Jozef, go to him," I say. "Ask him what has happened. I thought they agreed...."

Jozef, cigarette in hand, makes his way to the fire escape to see the judge.

"This is not good," Jawid says to me. "Not good."

Something out of the corner of my eye makes me turn. As I do, I see the TV camera pointing directly at me.

Jozef returns and says, "He will not talk to me. This is done, Ronald."

The judge enters the court and the cameras roll and he sits and produces sheets of paper on which his text has been written. He begins to read, reviewing first the testimony of the accused, what they had said on video, the evidence from the MOI and the girl. He speaks of the red car of Mirzo Muddin and how the three accused had received their orders to hunt down and kill UN people and how on July 20, 1998, they had successfully completed their mission. He then speaks of the debt Tajikistan owes to the UN and to the bravery of the peacekeepers. He then asks the accused to stand and says that he finds them guilty.

"The sentence now," says Jawid.

The judge speaks to each of the accused in turn and when he has finished, Jawid turns to me. "Death," says Jawid, "for each one."

The families in the court make no sound. The accused stand very still, but show no reaction. The judge stands, says it is concluded, and walks out. The camera rolls, following the judge, cutting to my face.

"When...?" It was all I could think to say to Jawid.

He shrugs. "Judge say as soon as possible."

"What was last night? The chief...."

Jozef says, "A game. Nothing. They were measuring our political strength and decided it was no threat. That is all."

We leave the court in a slow and sombre procession to the front gate, each of us reeling from what has just happened.

"I hope Bhatia is right," says Jawid.

It is not hard to understand that political decisions had been made to end the trial, and so it had ended and the issue was closed. The trial had become a nuisance and needed to be stopped before it became an embarrassment. If solid alibis had been allowed to be spoken, a guilty verdict beyond reproach would have been harder to attain. Then why have the trial at all? The outcome is a strange and inconsistent conflation of politics and law and order in a land of chaos and mayhem. Institutions cannot function in such a climate, with political whims cloaked in judicial robes. I have been naive to think they could.

When finally outside the prison we see that the crowd of relatives of the accused has gathered closely together. They are staring at us, but in silence now without any gesture or other indication of their mood.

I take my seat beside Jozef in the Land Cruiser.

"It is finished now," I say to him for lack of anything better to say.

"No. Our car light has been smashed. They are angry, these families. It may have just started."

As we drive away from the prison feeling ridiculous and sick, I sense the cold stares of the families of the accused on us. We cannot allow these men to die, guilty or not, is all I can think. On this issue, the United Nations must wield some power.

THEY ARE TRYING TO KILL US

(Dushanbe, Tajikistan—March 1999)

"Ron, here's the situation," says the UN Security Chief. We are sitting alone atop the UN main building in the bar built by the staff with money we raised to maintain our mental health. New York had sent shrinks to meet us and assess our psychological well-being. They reported that we had problems, living in fear and isolation, and so they sent other shrinks to help us cope. At one session of the latter, the New York shrinks drew Venn diagrams on an overhead projector to demonstrate how stress grew from a failure to establish sound coping mechanisms. They suggested watching the locals to understand which kind of behaviour best suited life in Dushanbe.

A veteran peacekeeper put up her hand. "The locals don't stay out after dark because they know someone will try to rob or kill them," she said. "They stay at home and worry."

The stuttering began. "Well, ah, yes.... Well, there must be something you can think of to alleviate the stress."

"They are trying to kill us," she said.

"That may be a slight exaggeration."

"Garm is dead!"

The psychiatrists or psychologists left Tajikistan recommending that we be given more funds to build an off-duty activity room on UN premises for the staff to use for positive play time outside work. Ping-Pong was suggested. We took the money and built a bar and got drunk, a lot.

The Security Chief is newly arrived to Tajikistan. He is an Irish national who has served in the Middle East and is, at this moment, very concerned.

"I am not havin' you or Jozef risked now that this is over. Your faces were plastered on TV. They broke the light of your car.... These boys are going to die. The families may try to take one of you as hostage. I've seen it often. No, you have to go and go now."

"I think that's overreacting. Besides, I'm scheduled to leave the mission in a few weeks anyway."

"I don't care. I want you out now. Tonight, if you can. You don't know. These three fighters are to be killed, after what you say was a sham of a trial. People get killed here for honking their horns too loud, Ron. No, I've spoken to our political types and we agree, for your safety, you and Jozef have to go."

"What about Jawid?"

"He is a local. He will have to take care of himself. But I will try to get him work out of Tajikistan, if he wants."

"When do you want me out?"

"Now. Tonight. Tomorrow at the latest. Quietly. I'm told we are surrounded by spies."

I am taken out of Tajikistan several days later on the same plane that had brought me in, a Russian Topolov four-engine propeller plane, without fanfare or ceremony and after saying a few quiet goodbyes.

"I am not worried," Jawid says to me at his home where we meet for lunch on the day of my departure. "I have no value to them."

We embrace in a Tajik farewell and I leave him, and the country, and the men now convicted of killing Team Garm to their fates.

I am exercising privilege, and I am leaving.

IT'S POLITICS

(Toronto, Ontario—April 1999)

Once back in Toronto I call the UN in New York to follow up on the three men convicted of killing Team Garm and to find out what steps the Secretary-General's office has taken to protest the conduct of the trial. Throughout the course of the investigation and trial, I had sent daily reports to New York to update the UN Tajikistan desk of what was transpiring. As the conduct of the trial judge clearly violated the basic standards of due process, I expect a strong response from New York.

A UN political desk officer for Tajikistan calls me back. She tells me that the Secretary-General had written to the president of Tajikistan asking that the death penalty for the men be commuted.

"That's good news," I say.

She then hesitates. "Something else."

"What is it?"

She tells me how she had taken my reports and submitted them to the Secretary-General's office for action. The Tajikistan political section within the UN proposed sending a letter to the president of Tajikistan requesting that the death penalty be commuted and expressing concern over the conduct of the trial. She then explains how the UN legal section had obtained the reports and drafted their own proposal for the Secretary-General to sign, which he did. It had already been sent to Tajikistan, she tells me. The letter did ask that the government commute the death sentence to life imprisonment. However, it made no reference to the glaring procedural improprieties in the trial. It is a silent acquiescence to a distorted process that resulted in three men being found guilty and sentenced to death.

I am too stunned to say a word to her.

"I'm sorry, Ronald," she says. "It's politics."

MONSTERS ARE REAL

(Toronto, Canada—2005)

A night in Phnom Penh in 1993, several months before the first free Cambodian elections are to be held. A restaurant has opened, selling hamburgers and french fries with a vague resemblance to what you can find at any fast-food restaurant anywhere in the world. They have even marketed themselves using an overlarge *M* as the first letter of their name. Located in the Vietnamese quarter of the city, the brightly lit and sparkling new interior is in sharp contrast to the grey and poorly lit noodle stands and cafés in the area. On this night, the cafés and noodle stands are full, with tables bursting out into the street, every chair occupied. I am sitting inside the M, eating soft ice cream, scarcely believing my luck. It is a hot night, like all nights in Cambodia, but by sheer good fortune the generator grinds along outside this establishment and the electricity is strong enough to run the icebox that freezes the ice cream. Outside, a rice seller's batons clack together, sounding like cicadas, and down the road, Vietnamese are clustered at their tables around flickering candles, laughing in the delight of freedom under the stars. Battalions of heavily armed UN peacekeepers are in the country and now, for the first time, everyone is safe.

Half way through my ice cream, I hear a heavy, slightly muffled bang from outside the restaurant. A motorcycle races by the window, two riders leaning hard into the ride, *krama* scarves flapping like flags behind them. The sharp and jarring report may only have been the motorcycle backfiring, I think to myself at first. But people on the street are running and then I hear screams, and know that it is not the bike that made that sound. I stand and walk out with ice cream in hand. Across the road, in one of the Vietnamese noodle cafés that had its chairs filled with nighttime revellers, there is now a scene of destruction. Most of the tables are overturned; dozens of patrons who had, moments before, been slurping noodles and laughing, now lie in ever widening pools of blood. There are screams. There is movement from some of the bodies, dragging themselves over the broken glass. I stand and stare and am unable to understand what I am seeing. These are movie scenes, or photographs I am looking at in a book. None of this is real. Rivulets of blood are forming around where I stand, but I cannot seem to move my feet to avoid them. The ice cream is melting over my hand.

Around the circle of the café, people are staggering away, clutching at themselves, at others. I hear shouting and other motorcycles racing down the street. A young man approaches me, holding out his arm. He wants me to see, to see the line of black dots along his bicep and the smudges of blood running down from each dot.

"Grenade," says a voice near me. I turn to see an Australian soldier I had come to know, who is standing, like me, on the outer circle of the café. "His arm has shrapnel," he says, pointing to the young man's arm as though to a rugby injury.

I am unable to move, my ice cream dripping into the blood at my feet. The mass of bodies in the centre of the blast, where the grenade must have landed, is becoming visible to me. I can see individual faces, arms, legs. I can see the crater in a man's chest and the meat of his insides. I have to do something, but I still can't budge.

A woman drops to her knees near me. She is from one of the aid agencies. She is cradling a boy's head on her lap and stroking his hair. He is not responding and she starts crying. Looking up at me, she cries out, "Do something, for God's sake. He's dying."

From this point onward, my memory of that night falters. It is a vague and distant dream to me now. Someone else's life on a faded film, projected on a smoky screen, replayed inside my head. There are times when I think that none of it happened, that my memory of it is wrong—so far am I now removed in time, in place.

But then I remember the warm and sticky feel of blood on my hands, and I know that some parts of what had happened to me had to be real.

That night in Phnom Penh, loading the wounded onto lorries, blood became smeared on my hands and then congealed to a sticky, glue-like paste. I stretched out my fingers and opened my palms wide against the constraining feel of drying blood, then closed them tight, to feel the stickiness. I kept repeating this movement throughout the night, opening and closing my fingers, somehow enjoying the strange sensation. Weeks later, the blood long washed away, I continued to stretch out my fingers and pump my hand closed then open, searching for the stickiness.

There are moments now when I believe I can still feel the blood on my hands. I force my hands wide and then close them tight, and I remember.

I am back in Toronto, in the overabundance that is our culture. I have two children, Jack and Matthew, twin boys, six years old. My heart bursts with love for them. Sometimes, I can't stop hugging or kissing them. "Stop it, Daddy," they say, pushing me away.

I will do anything to keep them safe, to make them happy. Sometimes to do that I lie to them.

Monsters pervade the movies they watch. They get scared.

"Daddy! Mommy!" A scream in the middle of the night that can jolt me out of bed in a heartbeat. My wife and I are on our feet and into the boys' room. Jack is sitting up in bed. Matthew has the blanket pulled over his head.

"What is it, my darling?" Antonia asks, holding Jack as she gently strokes his face and head.

"Monsters, Mommy, monsters. Under our bed."

I get onto my knees and play the game of thoroughly checking.

"Nothing there," I say.

"They were there.... I heard them," Jack insists. Matthew hasn't budged, his head under the covers.

"Boys, listen," I say getting to my feet. "The movie you watched tonight wasn't real. You know that. Monsters aren't real. They don't exist. They can't hurt you."

Matthew pulls the blanket back and looks at me. "Promise?" he asks. It is the absolutely binding obligation in our house. A promise is a promise, we say, and is never, ever broken.

They are both watching me now, searching my face for reassurance. My heart is aching.

"I promise," I finally say.

On a reflex that I can't control I open my hand wide and close it tight to feel for a stickiness that isn't there.

I have lied to them. Monsters are real. I have seen them. I have seen what they can do.

POSTSCRIPT

In February 2000, the United States Department of State reported that the three men found guilty of the killing of four UN peacekeepers (Team Garm) stationed in the Qarategin Valley, Tajikistan had been put to death.

ACKNOWLEDGEMENTS

I owe a great debt of thanks to my editor Wayne Tefs. He was insightful, patient and rigorous and without his input, this book could not have happened. I am grateful to the staff at Turnstone Press; Todd Besant, Jamis Paulson and Sharon Caseburg, for initially agreeing to publish the book, for next having the patience to wait for me, and finally for doing a terrific job in all stages of the process. They are brilliant at what they do. I also want to thank Toni, Tom and Alina Schweitzer, Barbara Morris, Dorothy Martel, Amber Wilson and Craig Scott, for their time in reading early drafts. Their comments were invaluable.